A Journey of Reflections

Lucinda "Cindy" Ossola

Table of Contents

Dedication

I dedicate my literary work to:

Edie, my mom, and George,
my dad, who have given me life,
love and the will to always forge on.

Marth
always encouraging and supporting my work,
my energies and visions of life.

All those that have encouraged me to print
this manuscript of thoughts and reflections.

The Journey

The Journey has been long,
The road uphill,
The rocks and ledges have made me struggle,
My steps are slow.

I gaze up the road,
My sight is obscured by the many hanging branches and ledges.
I look to either side as I struggle step by step.
Under my feet I feel the course rocky ledge and small stones sinking into my feet.

As I move slowly and steadily upward,
I keep my eyes centered on where I am going.
I slowly, maneuver around all that obstructs my path,
gently pulling aside the hanging branches and crawling over the ledges.
I forge on.

I move into an unseen clearing.
It is quiet and peaceful here,
I feel the softness beneath my feet.
What is this place?
It wasn't in my first view.

As I rest a while and soak up all that the space offers,
I see a glimpse ahead of my first view.
I question, is this place my goal?
Or is this place just another shallow view, an imitation?

I struggle to resume my uphill challenge,
leaving this peaceful and serene place.
Again, my feet step out on the hard ledges,
giving into the stones penetrating my feet.
Do I have the strength and energy to forge on?
Is the reward worth the pain, the sweat and time?

I take a deep breath,
experiencing a second energy moving through my body.

A tingling sensation and release of power overcomes me.
I look up and a glowing luminary adds another jolt to my pace.
Is this the goal? Am I growing closer to the summit?

My steps are swifter, my breathing becomes lighter
as I move around the hanging branches and rocky ledges.
My anticipation is like a child looking forward to an embrace of love.
At last the glow grows stronger and the narrow way begins to widen.

I feel, the softness under my feet and a light covering my face.
A widening ray of warmth encumbers my body.
And a peacefulness of endless sight radiates in my view.
I stand in the open space and embrace all that I see,
knowing the journey was worth the price.

Into the Light

The road has been long,
I have become weary and tired.
Once clear images have become obscure shadows,
I struggle step by step,
Feeling a heavy weight around me,
Peering through the darkness my movement is slow,
In my memory ever searching for familiar ground,
Will the road come into light?

It has been long this road I am on,
Thinking – "Have I taken a wrong turn?"
Again, I search for familiar ground,
Seeing many different paths,
I hunt for the signs,
Hoping to recognize a way to bring me back into the path of light.

I forge on, stumbling sometimes,
Catching myself from falling,
Echoing in my mind – "Could I be lost?"
Reassuring myself, it is the road,
But, "Why do I feel the way I do?"
Stopping at another crossroad,
I peer deep into the darkness,
A mist lifts before me,
Like a curtain being drawn up.
The outside changes have brought the darkness,
The entire familiar had surrendered – to the curtain change,
I am on the right path now,
Recognizing the familiar ground.
The obscure shadows are clearer,
My steps lighter,
The curtain of darkness lifts to bring me now a glimpse of the light,
My view is like a crystal bowl,
The path steadfast, ever reaching toward the light,
Once sapped energy begins to flow and ignite me,
Footsteps underneath me hasten to bring the light closer.
I slowly step off the path into the light,
Bathing in its warmth,
Knowing the dark curtain of change will no longer obscure

Amazing Light

Amazing light,
Oh beautiful view,
what glorious sight,
that comes through.

Oh cloud of mist,
a barrier that hides,
the mystery of the day,
riding on the tide.

I gaze to see,
the starlight dew,
what can it be,
those crystals in the blue.

These pieces of light,
the silent air surrounds,
the merging in delight,
reveals what can be found.

At last I see,
what is abound,
and I know you will agree,
a beauty that is profound.

Glowing Sensation

I take a deep breath,
experiencing a second energy moving through my body,
A tingling sensation,
and release of power overcomes me.
I look up,
and a glowing luminary adds another jolt to my pace.
Is this the goal? Am I growing closer to the summit?

My steps are swifter,
my breathing becomes lighter,
as I move around the hanging branches and rocky ledges.
My anticipation is like a child,
looking forward to an embrace of love.
At last,
the glow grows stronger,
and the narrow way begins to widen.

I feel,
the softness under my feet,
and a light covering my face.
A widening ray of warmth encumbers my body,
and a peacefulness of endless sight radiates in my view.
I stand in the open space,
and embrace all that I see,
knowing the journey was worth the price.

Doorway

I sit in the court yard of my life,
thinking and pondering about my direction.

Many thoughts weave in and out of my thought process,
Bringing me back and forth like –
the sea drags the seaweed in and out,
Never reaching the shore, close,
but pulling the seaweed again,
aimlessly with each wave.

I search around through my inner chambers,
Trying to sort out all the collection of –
feelings, thoughts and experiences.
Like a person would sorts through the treasures of old wood and empty shells –
found in the beach sand on the shore.

Some things have special meaning,
Others bring a reminder of challenge and pain,
Still others remind me of the joyous times –
that have brought me to where I am today.

I search ever so clearly for the doorway -
that opens possibly a new insight and meaning to me.
It is a time of clarity for all the obscured hidden meanings.
There are many openings, leading to many avenues,
But how do I find the right one I should open?

Ever Changing

I gaze out upon the water's edge,
watching the endless motion,
the rhythmic sound,
and the ever-changing notion.
The rising and falling,
the lull and the roar,
the culmination of the sound,
and quietness of the water flow.
Every wave,
changing color,
dark into light,
smooth and endless swelling,
spilling into splashing white.
Listening to the message,
of ever-changing time,
the constant in and out,
the pulling of the sand grains,
under my feet.
Time is measured by the motion,
lost in the ever-moving wave,
pulling and pushing,
ending in a changing tide.
Is life like,
the ever-changing tide?
Always in motion,
pulling and pushing us
through time.

Breath of Life

Breathe in the new air,
Clear your mind,
Shake out the dust,
Feel a new beginning.

Every year,
You look for new words,
New energy,
New life to inspire you.

Today, you look at the image,
An image of movement,
A constant change,
A new day set in motion,

As you were born out of love,
God kissed your soul,
Placed that soul within you,
Breathed life into you.

You don't need to hide in a room,
Suffer from anxiety of being found.
You are graced with courage,
Step out into the light.

Only you can bring a breath of life,
Hope in the darkness and despair,
Reconciliation in chaos and anger
Unity in division and live for the common good.

You are called to bring healing,
Show compassion at every turn,
Reconcile yourself with others,
Remember the Spirit of God dwells within you.

The Rain

Oh, drops of rain,
blood from those who were once,
but now only remain,
as part of the rain.

The drops of blood,
beat out a rhythm of time,
to show, all you may do,
will at last on earth shine.

The sun does not have to shed its rays,
for the sun will always shine,
through the everlasting drops of time.

I am alive and will strive to obtain,
but I too, will share a part,
a part of the rain.

The Sea

There is a place where people go,
although it is somewhere that we all know.
It's something more to each alone,
a quiet place, maybe a home.

It is what some would say,
a place to think day by day,
a home for many who have gone astray.
This space of seclusion,
a hide away.

Although, it is common to many of us,
we know, it can be a place of trust.
To a stranger, it's beauty maybe captured,
alluring one to the depth of its rapture.

I speak, so plainly of this place,
for it lives within the heart of man,
as beauty that is at hand.

It is, of course,
that which God has given,
a place for us to see,
This place and space, I speak of, it is the sea.

The Mountain of Light

Mountain in the distance,
unique in every way.
Light of brightness,
shining upon it through the day.

Green of envy,
covering it as a cloak,
waters of blue,
streaming down its slope.

Joys of life within this domain,
peace of heaven on the terrain,
processes and products,
living in union, gathered together,
sharing this communion.

Life of such unadulterated mirth,
earth here cleansed from all its dirt.
Mountain of light,
beckoning to you,
time on earth filled with virtue.

The Joining Together

Two paths on separate routes,
descending into the world of unknown,
two people treading that which belong to them alone,
upon the highway of their individual life,
encountering toil and strife.

The city of inequity in which they dwell,
causing grief and their own part of hell.
These, who care for those impoverished by the city's plight,
fighting against those who prey upon the pauperized for delight.

Each alone are half the strength,
needed to hold fast against the strain,
encountered in this den of pain.

One day, they left for self-esteem,
to a quiet place it seemed.
Along their path, one morning frosted and cold,
they met by accident in a common place, I'm told.

They shared a word or two,
parting for the work, they must do.
One evening, later, their path merged,
as the waters of the ocean would surge.

They came unto each other,
no falsity of human kind,
joined together with an open mind.

A Creation

Deny us not, Oh Lord,
all the beauty you have created.
For feeling and knowing beauty,
we shall obtain a part.

I once was told,
"All that is good is beautiful".
But is that so?

For in forgiveness of the evil,
we, also find beauty,
aren't thou, the most perfect,
and, I, but a creation of yours?

The Northern Lights

You have shown us your glory,
you have displayed your power,
for through the dark sky of night,
you drenched it full of color.

You took the colors of emotion,
and placed them before their eyes.
To the eyes of the mortal,
you produced, what they cannot on earth.

You took the red from the hearts of those who love,
the green from those who are jealous,
placing them far above,
so, all can see.

From the heart of you, Oh God,
you placed the transition between the two extremes.

True Friendship

A true friend,
Sharing thoughts and views,
Kindness and compassion,
Honesty and truth.

Oh, how rare to have a friend,
A sounding post,
A reality check,
Cold hard truths revealed.

Do you have a true friend?
One taking you to task,
Filled with love,
Providing you opportunities for expression.

No anger or bitterness,
An opportunity to be better,
A growing process,
Mutual respect for each other.

Jesus shares harsh words,
A true friend He is,
Choosing a hard road,
A path of goodness.

Do you struggle?
Let Jesus remind you,
Walk the difficult path,
Each step you will not be alone.

Your journey,
Accompanied by a true friend,
A commitment of support,
Filled with boundless joy.

Night

Run as fast as you can!
For only the night shall catch you,
it shall close your eyes,
and make you whoa.

It is not the darkness that frightens,
only the unexpected,
but the light shall come without reservation,
to light what you may suspect.

A Little Portion

One little sun's ray,
lights the earth,
a drop of rain fills an ocean,
a cloud covers the sky,
and a tiny pain pierces the heart.

All brings beauty,
but still destroys,
when raged will darken,
wind will blow,
the ocean will wave,
and the hearts will know.

The time in life is short,
to enjoy that which is beauty.

Echo of the Past

Were thou a friend or stranger,
who has passed my way?
Are thou someone,
who I have seen or known another day?

If thou were a friend of mine,
then I have shared with thee - time.
If thou were a stranger to me,
then I, too, have spent time with thee.

I can only recognize thee,
by the words that thou speak unto me.
The words of understanding and care,
I know that I did share.

Familiar thou are in manner and speech,
but the meaning to me no longer can reach.
Thou said, "I am but a friend of thee",
but my memory clouded with falsity,
I cannot say, "thou are a friend to me."

Time has passed since thou have known me,
maybe, I have been afflicted by time,
that is why,
I cannot remember thee.

My Love

I love thee, life.
You are the softness,
and warmth of the earth,
the salty,
and wetness of the sea,
the distance,
and lightness of the sky.

Although, it cannot be,
I would want thee to belong to me.

Place in Space

If I were to leave this place,
I would fine emptiness and space.
If I were to climb a mountain,
I would find nature's surrounding.

If I were to travel to the city,
I would find poverty and pity.
If I were to tread by the sea,
I would find a voice that would be free.

But if I were to go to all three,
I may find a part of life that will be free.

Seasons

For which of the four shall you favor?

The spring brings forth birth,
a season of warmth from the tender earth.

The summer nourishes,
bringing hope to the seeds of springtime.

The fall shall take these processes,
their products into an endless wedlock.

But winter shall reserve,
and hold life in a cold preserve.

Are we so strong as to favor one,
disregarding the rest,
life would be done.

The Depth of Wandering

The quiet and empty street below,
each individual light, giving its glow.
No footsteps heard upon the concrete and clay,
nor are children overheard at play.

The stillness echoes only a motion of silence,
and a depth of loneliness reveals its presence.
Loneliness is the oneness of being,
or the seeming to be something.

Oneness is to be an individual,
knowing that only you can establish tranquility,
to be set a float in the great sea,
hoping someone will recognize that you are not free.

Yes, being alone is striving and self-containing,
moving through life and still remaining.

Time

Time is of importance to us now.
For what in life can be hurried?
It is so set that all things must involve,
a little patience and a little know how.

I wish, at times, I could speed,
all the rivers and all the seas,
but we know that we cannot,
for we are mortal and a little spot.

For placing a finger upon a frosted pane,
it shows how small, and how retained,
but our size through life is not measured,
but only assumed by deeds and pleasures.

We strive so hard to be just so.
Why?
Because society has told us so,
but we, who are such individuals,
always try to be original.

To The Seeker

Seek! For only you can find,
whatever that you desire in your mind,
in your heart you shall reach,
and hope for a little portion of each.

You shall tread a path not taken.
but do not fear,
you shall not be mistaken,
only look and hear.

It may be a mountain to the sky,
or a valley to hell,
but in my heart, I know,
only you shall obtain and dwell

What Can I Give?

For what can I give to you?
Is it something that will last?
Or shall it perish like the oncoming waves of the ocean?

Whatever it may be,
I want it to be something pure and something rare,
for so many things that are given,
are common – without true expression.

If I were to give you,
the salt of the ocean,
it would lack the water.

If I were to give you,
the earth,
it would lack the life,
it possesses.

For in the partialities of all things,
we lack the full meaning.

So, I shall give to you,
only peace of mind,
to obtain all that you can find.

My Friend

You have brought into my life,
inspiration that I had lost at one time,
a seed of drive to obtain,
what was almost lost, but still remains.

I have been able to create,
with such humble tools,
disregarding any rules.

The words have come so easy to say,
I am glad you came my way.

At times, we do not appreciate,
what we have,
when we realize all may be lost,
a drive from within shows us the cost.

I cannot express in words,
what I could say to you,
my mind has been confined,
by everyday toil and grime.

Life

Life, what is this you lay before me?
Can I hold it in my hand?
Is it all that I can, see?
Or just a portion of your land?

One must roam through time,
to know what I shall seek,
if it is a part of mind,
or just possessed by the meek.

I shall never know what is in store,
or who shall hold the key,
for every window, there is a door,
Something that I cannot see.

Upon appearance, it appears to be,
something soft and something free,
but in essence, it is neither soft nor free,
only a portion, a little part of me.

The Endless Struggle

Is everything we do in vain?
I can only say,
what we do will always remain.

It will live in the hearts of those,
who are nearby,
and in the hearts of those from afar.

We cannot measure our worth,
or the potentialities of all we do,
for it is not written or prescribed in our efforts,
it only comes forth in whatever we do.

We are often judged as being unfair,
by those that are critical,
but you see,
they are only cynical.

Life is as it has been for many years,
a long road,
an endless struggle,
remaining in the hearts of those,
who are so dear.

The Earth, Sea, Sky
Proportional to Each Other

The earth gives us our birth,
only a beginning,
it starts so slow,
it's course to grow.

It instills life into that which does not exist,
a spark of life for eventuality.
The sea shall take the spark,
washing it about.

Life filled with endless fears and doubts,
but do not falter,
it will be altered by the currents of destiny.

The sky shall take the currents,
moving to a higher place of final resound,
it possesses all that has been created,
sweeping them to heaven with an endless bound.

To remain with He,
who first sought and now has found.

Watching Over You

Remember me in the change of seasons.
Know my presence in the new life of spring,
the warmth of the summer sun,
the first crystal snowflake on your cheek in winter
and the bright vibrant colors of fall surrounding you.
Remember me in the quiet moments,
the rhythm of music,
my light humor and humble heart.
May my words bring you comfort.
When you look up at the vast sky,
see me in the ever-changing clouds.
Know that I am alive,
now, as your guardian angel
watching over you.

Life Changed Forever

911

A blue sky,
a peaceful morning,
an ordinary day,
daily routines of life.

Many unsuspecting souls,
enjoying their ordinary conversations,
people hustling about,
planning for the day.

Evil lurking in the air,
plans of destruction,
taking of human life,
precise planning of chaos.

God watching,
tears of mercy and grace,
open arms,
waiting to embrace all.

Out of the clarity of the day,
planes on an evil track,
ceasing the quietness and blue,
emitting darkness and fire.

The horror and fear,
hearts ripped open,
brave souls helping others,
compassion evolving for each other.

A day never to be forgotten,
a nation of tears,
a nation of compassion,
a merciful God.

A nation stunned,
shocked and in disbelief,
hearts torn by emptiness,
sights ever ingrained in memories.

Last good-byes,
Loss souls to evil,
Brave heroes in the dust,
Love for each other evident.

God in mercy,
Wrapping His,
forgiving and loving arms,
pull souls to Himself.

United abiding,
People joining together,
Rebuilding life,
Softheartedness in the rumble.

I look at the flag,
tears fill my eyes,
I remember,
a nation of pain.

In the midst of the dust,
a glow of light,
a structure of a cross standing,
a triumph of unity in this nation.

Reflecting back,
Are we still unified?
If not, what are you doing,
to be part of the solution?

Am I Loved as I Am?

"Am I Loved as I Am?"
Interesting question,
Hard to discern sometimes,
Lost in deep contemplation.

Rising to this challenge,
Judging yourself,
Looking for many ways,
Seeking an answer.

What are your gifts?
Do you recognize your challenges?
How harsh do you want to be?
Obscured by your own skewed view?

You are loved passionately,
Unconditionally,
Loved forever from creation,
Guarded closely from harm.

You need to embrace being loved,
Beloved are you by your Father,
Leaving fear and judgment,
Recognizing this choice to happiness.

Bring your gifts and talents forward,
Make an ordinary life,
Extraordinary by your actions,
Let your belovedness grow in truth.

You need only ask for this grace,
Share it with others,
Experience your deepest desires,
Open your heart to being loved.

The Departure

Have you ever had to say, "Good-bye"?
It can be difficult,
sad or heart wrenching.
Times – forever or temporary.

What goes through you?
Do you remember the great times?
Is it a moment of relief from pressure?
Are you happy, sad or afraid?

The leaving can bring many thoughts,
An inner turmoil of feelings,
A wonder of an encounter again,
A moment of finality.

Does love end?
No, we gather the lessons,
Act with a love through our sacrifice,
We look for support.

In the peace of the departure,
We search for comfort and happiness,
The memories of the special moments,
The warmth of the genuine love elicited to us.

Are we worthy?
Can we be happy and joyous with our journey?
Staying focused on the departure.
Are we worthy to stand in the light?

Alleluia

No more darkness,
no soul lost,
new dawn of Hope,
tears of Joy flowing.

I promised you,
revealing the Father's plan,
opening the gates to the netherworld,
drawing you all to myself.

Do you believe?
Is it just for today?
Do you know I am present?
Do you know the depth of my love?

Yes, I have come for you,
I have opened my arms,
embraced each of you,
forgiven your sins.

I have dispelled the doubt,
brought light in my gloria,
made right the wrong,
opened the eyes of the blind.

I bring Peace to a world of unrest,
Living water to all,

Tides

The tides of life are like the rise and fall of the ocean,
experiencing, sometimes, the consistency of all things,
and, in turn, moments of devastating insecurity.

We are but complex entities,
set upon the waters of life,
changing as the tides change day by day.

You are far reaching from within your soul,
grasping for those things to keep you above the waves of destruction,
with the tow of endless motion into eternity.

You wander many times in search,
finding only that which you once left behind,
small treasurers kept within your mind.

Seashells along the shore,
castles built through ideality,
washing away like sand castles in the waves.

Life is encompassed with many tides,
high tides of fulfillment,
low tides drenched in despair.

Tides are of constant motion,
everchanging, bringing forth,
filling the empty parts of your life

A Time of Challenge

It is a time of challenge and uncertainty,
each day faced openly.
Imagine, how the challenges and uncertainty
look to our young people?
Role models, we are,
stemming the tide and waves of unrest,
guiding, young people, not to be overcome,
protecting against upheaval and risks,
daily challenges present to them.
It is difficult for everyone to look at change,
agreeing not,
looking for the evil, instead of, good.
Do you just throw your hands up in the air?
Are we all God's children,
loved so much by Him?
He was willing to sacrifice,
His only Son on a cross,
a sacrifice for eternity with Him.
Let us all move forward,
eliciting a positive attitude,
leading young people,
showing them,
working together,
for peace and harmony in the world.
Jesus gave us two great commandments,
"Love God with your whole mind, soul and heart and your neighbor as yourself".
God bless all of you and pray for all those that have no-one to pray for them.

New Hope

Where are you going to find Hope?
Is your path you travel the same?
Do you reflect on the same thoughts?
Do you see a New Light bringing a New Hope?

In the New Light,
you are encouraged to seek beyond the old ways.
Look to the revealing rays of the Light,
as it shows a new reflection of New Hope.

Where do you seek and find the New Light,
in your everyday activity?
We are encouraged to look beyond,
the clutter and mess of each day.

When you let the New Light,
illuminate your path,
and provide the warmth of faith and joy,
you will see the New Hope awaiting you.

Your path will be clear,
your peace will engulf you,
your joy will overwhelm you
and you will grow in Love.

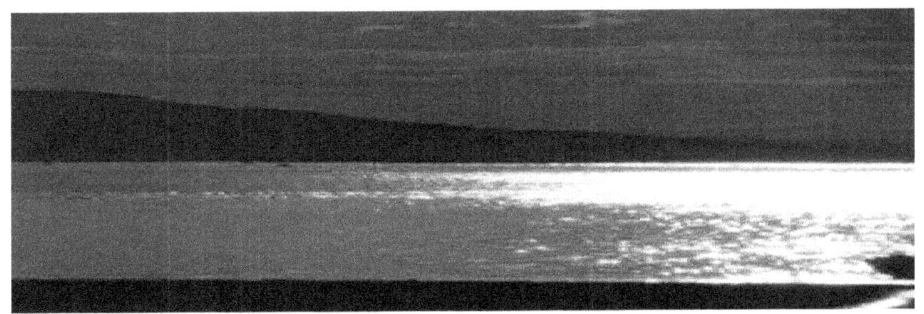

Be a Light

Be a light.
Shining bright,
A guide for others,
A way out of darkness.

We all share in the light,
We are all called,
Don't hide in the shadow,
Shine bright your light for others.

Despair, loneliness, hurt,
Push you into the darkness,
Feeling not whole,
Falling short and off the mark.

Engage with the encounter,
Be in the presence of the "Light",
Gather with others,
Igniting each other's light.

Being a light today,
Take courage,
You are a gift,
A gift of "Love".

Let not division and disconnect,
Dull your light.
Bring your beam,
Lighting a pathway to follow.

You are a light for others,
A moment or glimpse of brightness,
An avenue out of darkness,
"Hope" in a troubled world.

Being Satisfied

Are you satisfied?
Are you always looking for something?
Do things not bring joy?
Or maybe a temporary joy?

We look for joy,
Seeking happiness,
Not finding,
That lasting bliss.

What is wrong?
Are you filling your life up?
Filling your life with stuff?
Are you bordering on greed?

Rich or poor,
Greed can creep in.
Are earthly possessions important?
Then, where is God?

Greed never satisfies,
Only emptiness lies in possessions,
A false hope,
Never enough, lacking satisfaction.

Meaning and purpose,
Satisfaction and joy,
Fulfillment and happiness,
Lies in our Creator.

Ask God,
For a grateful and generous heart,
He will not disappoint,
And you will be satisfied.

Brokenness

Do you think,
we suffer from brokenness?
Look around you,
what do you see and hear?

Today, 9/11, what comes to mind?
A day of broken families,
Lost love ones,
A dark arrow,
Piercing hopes and dreams.

You experienced and questioned,
how could this be?
How did evil seep into our world?
How do you heal from such vulnerability?

Do you live in a bubble?
Did you think you were above reproach?
Now more battles are to be fought,
Others running away from oppression.

You are experiencing social upheaval,
A change in the norm of life,
People turning away from the Light.
What do you do?

How do you deal with the pain?
A complex problem is at hand,
Families and the world in turmoil,
Darkness blocking out the Light.

Christ's Light is at the center of our Hope,
Employ compassion and a forgiving spirit,
With your hands reach out,
Reach out in the darkness of all our brokenness.

Choices

You are faced with choices,
Small ones and larger ones,
Insignificant and serious,
Cheap and some expensive.

What of these choices?
Do you think about them?
Do you decide in a moment?
What weighs in for you?

Choices can be planned,
Deliberated for the future,
Others quick and short term.
How about your faith?

We are called for a decisive action,
Confronted by many choices.
How do you choose?
The choice is God alone.

In all the choices,
Give freely to others,
Express a concern for the salvation of all,
Be ready to sacrifice for others.

You say,
"Choices are too demanding",
Jesus says,
"Follow me and pick up your cross."

Curiosity

Curiosity,
an interesting term.
What meaning comes to you?
Does it bring back a memory?

You have experienced curiosity,
A sudden appearance,
A chosen path,
A glimpse recognized.

As a child,
You explored to learn,
An experience pleasant,
A path harsh filled with consequences.

You have discerned many situations.
What drew you to them?
Curiosity?
A wanting to know?

Curiosity elicits several results,
Moments of joy in finding,
Feelings of despair in revealing,
Reward in times of discovering.

Are you like Zacchaeus?
Wondering and curious about Jesus?
Amazed at the results,
Over joyed with the outcome.

You need to cultivate curiosity,
In the good with imagination,
Have faith in the fruits,
And embrace the rewards.

Do What You Are Asked?

Do you do everything,
you are asked to do?
Do you have a tendency,
to argue or dispute the request?

Are you aware of the needs of others?
Is an inner voice rationalizing,
what you see?
Do you take Jesus' examples to heart?

Every day, we get requests,
a family member, friend, or associate,
how do you respond?
What do you feel inside?

You see,
you are asked to respond with a loving heart,
a tender care for the needs of others,
a more compassionate attitude to serve others.

Jesus' words, "love one another,"
you are asked to be the love in the world,
to fill the empty plate,
and bring hope to the downhearted.

You are asked,
asked to be open to the Holy Spirit,
inviting you to share yourself,
offering your gifts with mercy.

In Christ's love,
you are asked,
be a friend,
be a light in the broken world of darkness.

Do You Bear Fruit?

Do you bear fruit?
Seems like a silly question?
Not really,
You are a child of God.

We are all called to holiness,
We are all call to bear fruit,
Accompanied by good works.
Do you need another year to be fruitful?

When we love someone,
A model,
They become,
Our desire to be like them.

Do you love Jesus?
Enough to be like him in the world?
To fertilize the barren soil,
Cultivate the bare tree.

We are gardeners,
Working the soil,
Planting the seeds,
Nourishing the roots of faith.

As Christ becomes more in us,
We become less,
He nourishes us,
So, we bear good fruit.

As we are being transformed,
We remain in our appearance,
But inside,
Our spiritual self-moves to holiness.

Do You Have the Time?

A question asked often,
"Do you have the time?"
Is life swallowing your time,
Struggling daily for space?

Wrapped up,
Discerning many things,
Trapped in a tight space,
Wanting a breath of air.

You are challenged,
Pulled in every direction,
Wanting more,
Sometimes less.

What is important?
Important to you or others?
How to prioritize all these feelings?
Who is calling you?

You discern,
Discerning only in authenticity,
Brings a true light to your chaos,
Jesus invites you into authenticity.

You are called to commitment,
Evolving out of discernment,
Assisting you to be grounded,
Grounded into who you are.

Faithfulness

What is faithfulness?
Do you have a responsibility?
Is it a focus on Jesus?
How far will you go?

There are many unsurmountable tasks,
Challenges indetermined or undefined,
A rocky path,
Rough waters with cloudy depths.

Where do you turn?
How do you maintain your focus?
Is the task impossible?
Do you wither up and turn your head?

It is easy to walk away,
An out of sight,
Out of mind experience,
Or a loving compassion heart.

Do you question your presence?
A feeling of unprepared,
An ill-equip focus,
A what difference would you make?

We are reminded,
Focus on what you have,
Your knowledge, skill and loving heart,
But more so focus on Jesus.

Jesus will provide,
Just ask Him, tell Him,
You can't do this without Him.
Jesus will reward your faithfulness.

Grateful Heart

What is it to be humble?
Do you find humility easy?
You probably shake your head,
Wondering the true meaning.

Understanding yourself,
Searching through your emotions,
Reaching conclusions,
Pondering the true sense.

Look at your blessings,
They are gifts,
Understanding the source,
Unearned or entitled – humility.

Are you appreciative of your gifts?
Can you be honest in your feelings?
Integrity is a key,
Humility is the door to gratitude.

In faith,
We receive God's gifts,
Each breath, each day and each night.
You were created as a gift!

What gift do you have to give in return?
Only a conversion of your heart,
Understanding who you are in God's eyes,
experiencing God's mercy and forgiveness.

To be humble is difficult, an endless task,
Falling short in your response to God's love,
You ask, God teach me humility,
Grant me a more grateful heart.

Essential Water

Essential water,
Holy Spirit,
water of rebirth,
new life in God.

When you bless yourself with Holy water,
do you think about what transpires?
Is there a significance in your action?
Do you know it is a prayer? A renewal?

God strengthens us,
gives us fortitude,
renews are hope,
reminds us of our Baptism.

Jesus was baptized,
given strength,
strength against temptations,
temptations of the evil one.

Jesus,
let us be renewed,
experiencing the joyous occasion,
being born out of Holy water.

Jesus,
let us experience,
the strength, fortitude, and hope,
given through the protection of the Lord.

May we be reminded,
upon blessing ourselves with Holy water,
our Baptism and rebirth,
through the power of the Holy Spirit and this essential water of life.

Beyond Sweets

Another year has passed,
anything change for you?
Are you right back,
thinking about the same thing?

The journey begins,
The walk with Christ,
To the cross.
Is it going to be different?

Yes, we need to fast.
Is it sweets again?
How did you do last year?
Any satisfaction?

Fasting goes "Beyond Sweets",
We are so blessed,
We have so much to give,
Or so much we can give up.

Sharing our blessings,
Reaching out to others,
Letting power or privilege go,
Making life better.

We have an opportunity,
To reflect on our privilege and power.
How are we using it?
Can we make the change, putting God first?

This is a time to reset ourself,
A time to reflect on our gifts,
A time to thank God,
Using our gifts for God and others.

Begin Again

How often,
Do we try to start again?
Are there many things,
We attempt to do right?

Feelings of unworthiness,
Attempts abandoned,
Shortcoming frustrations,
Loneliness in an abyss.

Yes, do we see only the darkness,
The lack of completeness,
A half empty glass,
An aching heart?

We know,
There is a power to begin again.
A forgiveness, a comfort,
A peaceful beginning.

A beginning,
A new slate,
An empty page,
A light in our darkness.

Yes, look to begin again,
Reach out of yourself,
Look to the half full glass,
The completeness that could be.

Jesus, I reach toward you,
Opening up my heart,
Embracing your mercy,
Drinking up your forgiveness in this new start.

At Your Gate

Who is at your gate?
Do you notice them?
Are you too busying with life?
Are you chasing riches?

It is easy,
Wrapping yourself up,
Looking beyond,
Not seeing in front of you.

You schedule your days,
Breathing not,
In constant motion,
Wondering where time goes.

You have many blessings.
Are you satisfied?
Do you share these?
Do you look beyond yourself?

God sees the suffering,
He sees those with blessings.
Do you create a chasm,
between God's desires and yours?

Reach out,
Help the less fortunate,
Grow closer to Christ,
Experience a personal encounter.

Open your door,
Welcome the less fortunate,
Bring Christ to them,
Rest peacefully.

Ask

Do you ask?
Does it make you feel uncomfortable?
Are you shy about it?
Do you discourage the effort?

To ask,
Many questions evolve,
Fearful thoughts,
Afraid of no.

Do you feel,
this is a rude action?
"Am I infringing?",
What will the response be?

In asking,
Assess your need,
In knowing,
It will be easier to ask.

Conversations ensue,
Clarification emerges,
Peacefulness will blanket you,
Anticipation of fulfillment will arise.

When you ask,
Unexpected reassurance is given,
You will know,
It is not selfish.

God and others,
Offer an embrace of comfort,
Asking and receiving.
Gifts given in love.

Are You Cut Off?

When you hear the term, "cut off",
What comes to your thoughts?
Being isolated?
No-one liking you?

Being cut off,
Elicits many different meanings,
For some – isolation,
For others – not being included.

Thoughts can bring on distractions,
Times when you are drawn to other places,
Loss of concentration,
Stray thoughts in the menial tasks of the day.

You are called to pay attention,
To be alert,
To know and feel the presence of God,
A glimpse in the view or another.

You are placed within a world,
Elements bombarding you,
Sometimes serious situations,
Uncontrollable moments.

You can drift through,
Oblivious to God's presence,
Creating an unchanging world,
Experiencing the same results.

Opening your vision,
Seeing the presence of God,
Embracing the view,
And watch your world slowly change.

A Humble Heart

What is a humble heart?
Have you ever thought about it?
Are you too busy being important?
How do you view others?

Entering a room with others,
Looking around to see who is there,
Where do you fit in?
Maybe you don't fit - at all.

Are you conscious of others?
Seeing if they are comfortable,
Listening with a humble heart,
Guiding others to importance.

We are called,
Sometimes to be last,
Not first,
To be unimportant.

Courage prevails,
Opening your heart to everyone,
Not judging or disapproving,
Accepting and helping.

Do you have a humble heart?
Can you view your surroundings?
Looking through the eyes of God,
Are you willing to assist no matter the status?

Listen to the voice of God,
Beckoning you to act,
Calling you to reach out to the poor and
marginalized,
This, we call a humble heart.

A Quiet Voice

Listen attentively,
Move slowly through the times,
Moments of confusion and struggle,
Trust in the quiet Spirit's voice.

Can you hear it?
Can you feel God's grace?
Are you experiencing the forgiveness?
Jesus making things new.

Can you truly forgive?
Loving your enemy,
Loving your neighbor,
Setting aside your feelings.

Will you love someone
that has trespassed against you?
How can you be loving and fair?
Will your heart be open?

Jesus offered Peter,
A way back from his denial,
A moment of forgiveness.
Your life guided by Jesus' example.

As you share in the bread and wine,
Jesus' body and blood,
May you be strengthened by these gifts,
May you live a life with love in your heart.

Listen to the quiet voice,
The Spirit encouraging you,
Directing you,
Guiding you toward God's grace.

A Beautiful Gift

A beautiful gift,
Given to each of us,
Unique in many ways,
Similar in some.

How can this be?
Such diversity,
Yet the same,
Sharing together.

It unfolds slow,
Filled with expectations,
Sometimes peacefully,
Occasionally with challenges.

You learn to trust,
You grow in confidence,
You surrender to pressure,
Seeing the truth.

You open the corners,
Looking for change,
Attempting to see,
But are blinded.

You have to trust,
Open your heart,
Grow in love,
Treasure each moment.

What have you been given?
A moment of breath,
A beating heart,
A kissed soul.

This "Beautiful Gift" - life from God.

Fear or Faith

We have seen God's unlimited love,
a sacrifice,
surpassing anything,
we can comprehend.

Why do we sometimes doubt?
Why do we fear?
Is it the unknown obscured from sight,
in fog with an anticipated view?

Do you have fear or faith?
Do you blindly believe?
Do you believe what is taught or seen?
Do you still question in times of sorrow?

In faith,
we open ourself,
to all God's gifts for us,
we embrace the challenges with an open heart.

In fear,
we hide in the shadows,
rationalizing why,
protecting and justifying our every thought.

Do you need to see, to touch,
to feel, to believe?

Can you believe, by faith,
by witness, by the cross?

May the Resurrection,
of our Lord, Jesus Christ,
open your heart to faith and belief.

Expectations

Do you wake with expectations?
Is your life filled with spontaneity?
Are you a person of Hope?
Do you witness life's Joy?

You know the story,
Jesus reminds us,
By the teachings of Hope,
The beauty of creation.

You look to the light,
A journey known,
Moments of unknown,
Overturned expectations.

Joining in community,
Experiencing solidarity,
Sharing with the marginalized,
Uplifting a sense of Hope.

You were created out of love,
A beautiful love,
Spoken into existence,
By a God of love.

Share God's world,
A sense of order,
A Hope and Joy,
Into the core of life.

Will You Leave?

The Eucharist,
Christ's Body, Blood, Soul and Divinity,
His presence to us,
living nourishment for our journey.

Would you have left him?
Disciples walked away,
not understanding,
they had to eat his flesh and drink his blood.

What does this mean to you?
Would you have left?
Do you leave today?
Do you feel Christ's real presence in you?

When Jesus presents a challenge,
do you trust in him?
When the truth is not easy,
do you walk away?

Lord Jesus,
life is filled with inconvenient times,
stir in me the trust,
the act of faith to follow you.

In the depths,
may I see your light in the darkness,
guide me toward you,
help me to understand this peace.

Jesus,
direct me to understand what you ask,
give me courage to follow you,
fill me with your living water.

Who is Your Shepherd?

Is violence winning over you?
Are you discouraged by abuse?
Do you feel neglected,
alone and in despair?

In this busy world,
who is your shepherd?
Who leads you?
Do you hear a call?

Jesus called both Jews and Gentiles,
beckoning them to follow him,
standing with open arms,
revealing the love of the Father.

Jesus draws us together,
showing us a way to reconciliation,
joining people of separation,
mending their differences.

Open my heart and mind,
draw me closer to your light,
use my hands and feet,
let me hear your words.

Oh Jesus,
help me to be your instrument,
working to mend,
a broken and suffering world.

What do You Wish to See?

What do you want to see?
A simple question,
filled with much meaning.
An answer in vision unexpected.

How often to we proceed in blindness?
Do we see what we want?
Are simple things complex?
Are simple requests unheard?

The faith of a simple beggar,
refusing to be silent,
calling out in his darkness,
looking for the light.

An answer from the light,
"What do you want me to do?"
The simple words,
"I want to see."

If the Son of God,
asked you this question,
what would your response be?
Would you ask to see better?

Surrounded by much darkness,
it is difficult to see.
Does your faith surpass all fears?
Will you speak out without fear of rejection?

Son of God,
strengthen me to see your vision,
reaching out in the darkness,
bringing your light to the forgotten.

What do I have to Give?

Lord Jesus,
through my baptism, I share in your light,
I am called to share this light with
everyone I encounter in my life.
What do I have to share?
What skills do I have like the first disciples?
How can I too be a fisherman of many today?
Am I skilled as they were to gather others to themselves?
Reflecting on the first disciples,
"Did they really understand your message?"
I too wonder,
if I can understand what you ask of me.
So, I have gone back to your teachings,
"How do I treat my neighbor?"
Do I love others as I love myself?
Do I love God above all things?
Reflecting brings me to a threshold,
loving others comes with a great price.
A price you paid a long time ago.
that comes only through forgiveness and understanding.
May I be a channel of forgiveness and understanding,
a beckon in the darkness of despair,
a light in the shadows,
a hand reaching out to others.
May I bring peace and love
to a world in turmoil and despair.
May my actions help to bind the wounds,
and open the doors of uncertainty.

Walking the Way

Believe in me,
don't be afraid and worry,
know that I am with you
and I love you.

Walk in my footsteps,
share the "Good News",
gather others into my light,
let them know of my love.

Jesus extends himself to us.
What kind of witness are you?
Do you search out the lonely?
Do you look for the sheep gone astray?

Jesus invites us to walk the way,
He knows,
the challenges we will face,
the moments of hesitation.

As you ponder the way,
in our time of history,
rest in Jesus' promise,
I will be with you always.

Walk in His footsteps,
breathe in the new Hope,
gather everyone into the light,
know Jesus is with you in every step.

May you embrace each day,
reaching out for those living in darkness.

Trust in Jesus

Is your life cluttered,
filled up with many messages?
Are your senses confused?
Do you not know the way to turn?

Opinions reeking of their points,
amounting to "two cents",
discerning what you hear, see or experience,
you are not alone.

Jesus shares what will happen,
a planet out of control,
an end in the final days,
fear struck within his disciples.

What will this world be like?
Imagine a catastrophic impact,
many sufferings,
a world no more.

Jesus reminds us,
why he came,
who is,
what he has taught.

Do we lose sight in our busy life?
Is all the clutter,
distracting,
causing us to lose our focus?

Jesus, may we remain,
focused on your hope and trust,
your ever presence in the Eucharist,
and live-in the faith of the good news.

Jesus may our faith be solid,
knowing you have our backs always.

Transformation

Do you believe in change?
Is it noticed by you?
Can you feel it?
A soft tug on your heart.

Jesus's flesh,
the bread we receive,
His life given for the world,
our nourishment for the journey.

Do you feel changed by His presences?
Are you alive and strengthened?
Christ changes us,
transforms us to be Christ in the world.

Are you ready to be consumed by others?
Our communion transforms us to be Christ's body,
sent forth to be broken and consumed,
sharing a self-emptying love in the world.

Your Amen,
directs you and nourishes you for the mission.
Yes, your mind, heart and flesh are offered,
you are offered to a world in hunger for Jesus.

Lord, Jesus,
continue to strengthen us for the task,
help us to carry the cross against skepticism,
denial and the evil.

Holy Spirit,
Give us the words and prayers,
the inspiration to offer Christ's light in the darkness,
the heart and courage to live our "Amen."

Thoughts of Anticipation

My thoughts turn to this new day.
What will be sent my way?
Will I rise to the challenge?
Will I engage with love?

In the morning,
sunlight opens my eyes,
seeing all you have created,
being thankful for this day.

I reflect on this gift,
a new beginning,
anticipated meetings,
a hope for meaningful encounters.

Every breath,
gives a full meaning of life,
soft sounds,
tune my hearing into you.

You gave me many gifts,
moments of blessings,
times of quietness,
comfort of warmth and security.

I move through this day,
a joy of anticipation,
a smile of encountering love,
arms open wide to embrace all.

May I be filled with your presence,
knowing at the fall of sunlight,
you are surrounding me,
in your loving embrace.

Suffering Servant

Are you like the disciples?
Peter knew the answer,
or did he?
Is it painful to understand truth?

Jesus reveals,
I am a "Suffering Servant",
not a powerful king for you,
I will greatly suffer.

Will you follow in His footsteps?
Do you see Jesus' way?
Can you be merciful and loving?
Marks of your true faith.

Understand Jesus' way,
become a true servant,
build a relationship with Him,
and bask in the glory of the resurrection.

Lord Jesus,
I long for a closer relationship with you,
I pray for greater trust and faith,
open my heart to experience your love.

May the power of the Holy Spirit,
open my heart to the wonders of God,
be a "Suffering Servant" like you,
finding meaning and purpose in a broken world.

Spiritual Intentions

Sometimes, do you feel like a pew sitter?
When God calls you to follow,
do you jump up?
Are you a doer of God's word?

What drives your spiritual intention?
Are you authentic?
Do you recognize the theme of obedience?
How do you show true devotion to God?

Many questions, but where are the answers?
Embrace your source of faith,
a heart filled with love and mercy,
a true spirit of hope.

Even though,
emptiness can loom,
there are misplaced intentions,
losing sight of our true spirit.

We worship through rituals,
enhancing our experience,
soaking into our spiritual souls,
the love of Christ's presence in us.

May God's gifts to us,
draw us ever close to him.
May we follow Jesus,
with pure intentions and actions.

Season of Peace

We speak of Peace.
What is Peace to you?
An absence of struggle
or quietness with rest?

When we were young,
life was simple,
we traveled many roads,
but age brought us,
many hard and decisive choices.

Today, we sit on the brink,
always at a crossroads,
always struggling with choices,
exhausted and tired.

We hear John saying,
"Repent!"
What does this word mean to you?
Maybe a change of Lifestyle?
Could a new path,
a new road,
a different choice brings a new way?

Jesus,
challenge us,
leading us to a different path,
one with Peace and reflection.

Pray for Jesus' guidance on your journey,
keeping you ever steadfast.

Season of Love

What is love?
A moment of passion,
a conditional relationship,
terms drawn up between two people?

Mary showed us,
faith and love of God,
trusting beyond,
knowing the consequence of her time.

Have you prepared yourself?
Are you opening your heart?
Do you have the faith of Mary?
Are you trusting beyond control?

As Christmas grows nearby,
will you experience,
the love of God?
Will you be open to His love?

We wait for the Christ,
we have prepared our hearts,
our faith and love,
our trust in an unconditional love.

We pray, loving God,
trusting in you,
opening our hearts,
we turn to others,
Sharing the beauty of your love.

Season of Hope

Do you think about,
the Son of Man coming?
A predicted time,
without a date.

Advent,
the first week of Hope,
expectations and dreams,
heartwarming thoughts.

Will you be ready?
Will you stand erect?
How will you respond to Jesus?
Will life cloud your vision?

Be ready,
be watchful,
be alert,
be attentive.

This season is veiled by,
the hustle and bustle,
the gift buying,
the parties and comradery.

Look for a blend,
not losing sight of Advent,
a time of reflection,
a time of Hope this week.

Lord Jesus,
may I be watchful and alert,
attentive to the anticipation,
in anticipation of your coming.

Saying No to the World

We have heard,
"Be in the world,
but not of the world."
What does this say to you?

What is important in your life?
List the many things,
decide the importance of each.
What does your list look like now?

Where is God on your list?
Does the world take your time?
Are there other Gods more important?
Which God will you choose?

If you say yes to one thing,
is it no to many more?
If we make time for God,
it is a response to all the love he has shown us.

When we immerse ourselves in the Eucharist,
we truly build our relationship with Jesus.
Look to your gifts,
use those to enhance the Kingdom of God.

Jesus, I will take time for you,
pray and commit time to you,
moving you to the top of my list,
honoring and loving you in return.

Jesus,
may my relationship grow,
may I be an instrument of love in the world,
but saying no to the world.

Rooted in God's Love

Do you expect miracles?
Do you have the faith of a child?
Has Jesus healed you?
Do you feel his presence?

How often do you share your faith?
Do you look for those in need?
Do you ask Jesus to heal others?
Have you brought others to Jesus?

A blind man brought to Jesus,
those caring for others,
hearts and faith of children,
humble and ready for the wonders of God.

Have the childlike faith,
a heart open to others,
believe in Jesus' power,
a union with God, Father, and Holy Spirit.

Is your faith rooted in God's love?
Share what you receive,
bring forth the power of love and mercy,
a compassion wrapped in Christ.

God's love roots us in a merciful heart,
words, deeds and prayers,
healing and perhaps miracles,
bringing joy and hope to all.

Open your heart,
believe in the miracles,
share your faith,
love others with a child's heart,
and be rooted in God's love.

Remain in Me

When Jesus said,
"If you remain in me and
my words remain in you,
ask for whatever you want,
and it will be done."

Where do your thoughts go?
What is important to you?
Do you think about things that don't last?
Does your mind wander away from Jesus?

Are we distracted and weak?
We do need to believe,
our comfort and peace,
comes only through resting in Him.

Jesus,
I pray to always stay close to you.
I know only you,
can bring great joy and contentment to me.

I pray you will hold me,
close to your heart.
Shine your light of compassion,
understanding and mercy upon me.

I know in all my challenges,
remaining in you is all I need,
bringing strength and wisdom,
dispelling all my fears.

May I always remain and rest in you.
For only you,
can bring everlasting happiness and joy.

Reflecting on You

Alone on my journey,
I reflect on you, Jesus,
your journey to the cross
and all you endured.

I imagine,
your disappointment,
your hurt,
your abandonment by those close.

Following you,
your mother,
experiencing your pain,
wanting to protect you.

What were your thoughts?
Are my thoughts even close?
Watching each painful step,
feeling my heart throb for you.

Your journey,
ends in pain and humiliation,
a cruelty of suffering,
a death unimaginable.

What were your words at the end?
Forgive them, Father.
You knew of your glory,
and the prize for all of us.

My journey continues,
moving through the mountains
and valleys of my life.
Keeping always
your journey in my heart.

Peaceful Waters

Christ spirit and light,
Reach down,
Out of the darkness,
Illuminate the peaceful waters.

Peaceful waters,
Ever moving and unknown,
Make them known,
only through your light.

Christ,
Continue to illuminate,
These peaceful waters,
Bring a calmness and a new view.

May Christ light,
Bring us out of the darkness,
A darkness of doubt and despair,
Move us together in unity and trust.

May our faith in you, Christ,
Renew our journey,
Being Christ to each other,
Bringing light upon the peaceful waters.

Open Hearts

Lord Jesus,
Your Father,
made you known,
displaying you gloriously.

He challenged, Abraham,
sacrifice your son,
if you love me,
devoting yourself to me.

Our Father, blessed Abraham
sparing his son,
giving him descendants,
abundant as the stars.

How devoted are we?
How much love do we have?
If put to the test,
what would we do?

Lord Jesus,
we pray,
give us the strength,
know our love.

As we journey,
open our heart to your words,
protect us from all distractions,
affirm the words of faith, we speak.

Bless us and give us guidance,
we ask of you Jesus.

My Promise

No more darkness,
no soul lost,
new dawn of Hope,
flowing tears of Joy.

I promised you,
revealing the Father's plan,
I have opened the gates to the netherworld,
I draw each of you to myself.

Do you believe?
Is it just for today?
Do you know I am present?
Do you know the depth of my love?

Yes, I have come for you,
I have opened my arms,
embraced each of you,
forgiven your sins.

I have dispelled the doubt,
brought light in my gloria,
made right the wrong,
opened the eyes that cannot see.

I bring Peace to a world of unrest,
living water for all,
come and believe in my presence,
rest in my light.

I claim you for myself,
a light for the darkness,
a breath of life
you are my hands and feet in the world.

Trust in my love for you,
as I trust in your love for me.

Moving into the Light

Reflecting on my journey,
I see the up and down,
The level and flat,
The dry and wet of thoughts.

What have you seen?
Have you struggled?
Where are your steps going?
Do you see the light?

Reflecting on the down of darkness,
the up of joy,
the level of contentment
and the flat and dry of empty thoughts.

Do we want to remain in darkness?
Maybe living on the fringe of the shadows,
being seen and unseen simultaneously,
feeling the light and clarity,
still hidden in thoughts and actions.

Why hide in the shadows?
Move out into the light,
feel the warmth,
the unveiling truth of life.

Christ offers us the light,
a light to shine through us,
to bring clarity to the darkness,
to bring truth to the world.

Joined to you Christ,
through our Baptism,
may our light shine even brighter
at the end of our journey.

Mary's Trust in God

Mary's trust in God,
her faith abounding,
her steadfast strengthen,
seeing clear her call.

Do you have Mary's faith?
Would you have said yes?
What extent is your confidence?
Are you humbling enough to trust God?

Could her faith-filled response to God,
give you strength to say yes?
Can you carry Jesus today
openly into the world?

Inspire us, Blessed Mother,
assist us in our weakest time,
carry our prayers to your son, Jesus,
strengthen our confidence.

May we see you as our role model,
ever humble, steadfast and faithful.
May we embrace the cross your son carried,
being as faithful to the mission of love.

Mary, most holy,
may we experience God's mercy,
may we be faithful followers,
we ask this through your intercession.

Love One Another

Jesus said:
"Love one another
as I love you?"

How easy is this for you?
Do you think, "who falls in this group?"
Does Jesus mean, "Everyone?"
How do I love a stranger?

Reflect on Jesus,
He is the example and the Way,
going before us,
calling on us to follow in His footsteps.

What does it mean to love others?
Surrender to the moment of an encounter,
the exchange of a glance,
a word spoken in kindness.

Remember, we were created out of love,
others too are created out of the same love.
God holds us in our existence,
breathing life into us.

Every moment of each day,
search for the opportunity,
to love another,
bringing a smile and joy into their life.

Don't miss the opportunity,
you can be an instrument for God,
respecting and accepting others,
loving them as Jesus loves you.

Love one another,
as Jesus loves you,
and see the world change.

Love of Family

What is Family?
We all have definitions,
different reflections,
many memories.

Individuals,
coming together,
sharing together,
loving together.

What did God want for families?
At the beginning,
two people created for each other,
love generating happiness.

A love to grow,
blessings springing forth,
generations of happiness,
building memories for all time.

Love is the core,
a perpetual beat of life,
growing together each year,
smiles evoked from true happiness.

Love of family,
respect and kindness,
patience and understanding,
giving of oneself for another.

Lord, bless all families,
comfort the broken,
make whole the shattered,
let love become the core.

Looking to Jesus

Lord Jesus,
in our daily life,
we look to you,
for faith and trust.

A faith and trust,
in you knowing our need,
pains and sorrows,
never left unheard.

Your love and guidance,
brings us direction,
peaceful evenings,
hopeful mornings.

Resting in these thoughts,
we celebrate and praise you,
Lord Jesus,
lifting our voices in thanksgiving.

We celebrate your powerful grace,
a grace you shower on us,
giving us strength,
so, we can cry out for others in need.

May our voices and prayers,
echo throughout the halls,
our hands relieve the pain,
our compassion bring comfort.

Lord Jesus,
I look to you,
thanking you for all my blessings.

Trusting Jesus

How hard is it for you,
to know, serve and love Jesus?
How often do you turn from Him?
Do other things distract you?

When life gives you a curve ball,
do you abandon Him?
When things get tough,
do you take the easy way?

When Jesus answers your prayers,
does this restore your faith?
Does it take answers you want,
to return to Him?

Jesus offers you,
forgiveness, mercy, unending love.
He even gives Himself, to nourish you,
asking nothing in return from you,

Surrender to Jesus' divine mercy,
embrace the grace sent your way.
Have patience and faith in Him,
experience a new self, filled with trust.

Lord, Jesus, I trust in you.
I walk in your light,
no matter the challenges of my cross,
I rest in your divine love and comfort.

Living Tabernacle

How do you live each day?
Do you look at faith,
as a list of precepts?
What is your relationship with the Trinity?

When you receive Jesus,
does He nudge your heart?
Do you respond humbly to Him?
Do you feel united to the Mystical Body?

Our one baptism,
marks us as a follower of Christ.
Our one faith leads us to love,
a love of God and others.

We are the living organism,
attached to Christ on the cross.
In receiving His blood, body, soul and divinity,
we are the living tabernacle sent into the world.

Jesus, your body is the mystery of your love,
your real presence on earth,
bringing us into a deeper relationship with you,
with a desire to be your living tabernacle.

Jesus Christ,
you nourish me,
you strengthen me,
you give me the faith to share the "Good News".

May you give me the strength and desire,
deserving of your love,
an instrument of your grace and mercy,
as I share your words and love in the world today.

I Have Come for You

I have come for those in darkness,
a light of hope at dawn,
peaceful rays of comfort,
a lasting consolation.

Today, I come for all of you,
bringing my Father's mercy and compassion,
enlightening the ignorant,
exposing the falsehood.

I rest my hands on the isolated,
gathering them to my side,
sheep to the shepherd of everlasting life,
a place for everyone.

I will lead with humility and courage,
reassuring you of the Father's love,
knowing all are sinners,
only mercy and tenderness will prevail.

I have come out of love,
a love deeply rooted in your humanity,
an example of a new freedom,
a time and place of joyful eternity.

May I have the strength, Jesus,
to be as brave as you are,
facing all challenges and burdens,
I encounter in my life.

How Deep is Your Faith?

When all is well,
how deep is your faith?
When you get challenged,
how deep is your faith?

Jesus said,
"Don't be afraid; just have faith."
How do you respond?
When we see a loved one suffer,
do we pray in faith or ask God why?

In sickness,
are we sure that God will help?
Do we curse God,
asking, "why me" or are we reassured in his presence?

If we lose someone close to us,
is our faith shaken
or do we turn it over to God?
Do we feel his arms around us?

We are people of faith,
a people of hope and gratitude,
we immerse ourself in the words Jesus spoke.
"Don't be afraid; just have faith."

Jesus, you know the love of the Father,
you taught us His mercy and forgiveness,
you ask us to have faith,
a faith you showed to us on the cross.

May we all embrace your words,
take them to our hearts,
knowing that you will be there,
always to the ends of our earthly journey.

God's Powerful Love

When things are different,
how do you respond?
Are there two roads to consider?
Is it a test of faithfulness?

Are you drawn into a union?
If so, what is the relationship?
Are there boundaries for your love?

God draws us,
there are always two roads,
a union beyond human capacity,
a faithfulness of never-ending love.

God beckons us,
calling us to him,
His road and not the human one,
a bond unbreakable.

A self-gift in the cross,
a faithfulness to the end,
a love so powerful,
revealing the Father's love.

God's relationship to us,
going beyond any known bond,
a union so close,
a one in being.

A powerful love,
flowing into other life,
gathering them through us,
a peacefulness, a dawn of new light.

God is Calling

Have you heard God calling you?
Do you only listen,
when you need something?
Do you block out that Spiritual nudge?

We see many in history,
responding to God's call,
a wholeness in being,
by trusting in God.

Do you have dark days?
Many saints experienced the same,
trusting in God,
brought fruitful life action.

In your quiet moments,
turn to God,
trust in the Spiritual nudge,
let your heart be moved and opened.

Our culture,
brings unrest and stress every day.
You must first overcome your obstacles,
listen to the voice deep inside.

God is calling,
offering you a better way.
You can be the instrument,
to show a better way,
through your sacred wholeness.

A Gift

What gift do you possess?
Is it something you can give away?
Do you hold it dear and close?
What do you think God would say?

The rich man was sad,
unable to part with his possessions.
Are you too astonished by Jesus' response?
What would you do?

We have so many possessions,
many objects and things,
significant and insignificant,
old and new.

Sometimes, we curse these things,
space taking,
extra work,
clutter massing our life.

What deeper freedom is there?
Sharing these worldly possessions,
for the sake of others,
responding to the growing gap in our world.

God will call on us,
furnishing an account in the end,
examining our inner hearts,
our love and generous hands.

What of the gift?
Can you give yourself,
as a gift to others?
An unselfish and selfless living gift of love
or will you walk away?

Desert Journey

Lord Jesus, connected to you,
I'm your living organism,
journeying into the desert.

In reflection,
How can I draw nearer to you?
What will the wilderness reveal?
Where will I go to be closer to you?

I'm here, to see, hear,
open my heart,
absorb all you will reveal.

Heavenly Father,
reveal the paths,
the challenges,
my shortcomings.

Comfort me on this journey,
bring your light into darkness,
reassure me with your words.

Lord Jesus,
knowing your ever present,
reveal your ways,
guide me on this desert journey.

Common Good

What is "Common Good?"
Where do we fit into this?
Are there those set above this?
Is special privilege more important?

Jesus reminds us,
true leadership,
a servant leadership,
rises above.

"Common Good" is achieved,
accomplished by,
realized by the cross,
and support for the weak.

James and John,
bold and expected,
not truly understanding,
the nature of the kingdom.

How often do we misunderstand?
Is power where you side?
Like the disciples,
are our views distorted?

Jesus,
guide our views and thoughts,
enhance our servant heart,
let us look for the "Common Good."

Jesus reminds us,
it is important to serve,
to reach out to the lowly,
lift up and protect the vulnerable.

Lord, Jesus,
may we follow you,
may we emulate you,
may we look for the "Common Good."

Do You Believe?

Are you like Thomas?
Do you need to put your fingers
in Jesus' side?
How deep is your faith?
Do you struggle when you don't see?

Faith is a precious gift,
a gift needing constant care,
a searching of your heart,
needing time for rest and quiet.

A new dawn has passed,
time for joyful jubilation,
doors opened in peaceful calm,
a breath of freshness surrounding.

Search for truth,
explore your convictions,
usher forth what you believe.
recognize the truth God reveals.

In days of threatening trials,
moments that overwhelm your tolerance,
turn to Christ,
receive His abundant grace.

Believe not because you see,
but believe because Christ promised you.
Believe with a heart of faith,
a joy of overwhelming grace.

Born of Spirit

Born of Spirit,
a new life from water,
a child of God,
emerging from inherited sin.

Holy Spirit,
guide me,
bring light into my day,
direction into my journey.

Where there is doubt,
reassurance.
Where there is hesitation,
solid decisions.

In time of anticipation,
a hope and clarity,
times of decisiveness,
and secure thoughts.

Breathe in me,
Holy Spirit,
life and vision,
strengthen and wisdom.

Bring me closer to you,
through guided understanding,
instances of counsel,
and a life of love and charity.

Coming to the Lord

I come to you each time,
opening my heart,
opening my mind,
opening my soul to your presence.

I pray to have the words,
the acts desirable,
positive thoughts toward others,
and a contrite heart.

I pray,
you gather all my joys and sufferings,
placing them with those of the world,
and at night, place me with your Mother.

I gaze at you in my hands,
telling you of my love,
I have only for you,
My inner thoughts reaching out to you.

I embrace you,
kiss you silently,
I pray for your strength,
to encompass my soul.

As you journey,
into my depths,
I feel your presence,
your life-giving power.

Securely I know,
you will be there,
strengthening me
and being a light of grace.

Being Open to God

As I journey with my cross,
thoughts and reflections,
fill my mind and heart.
How open am I to you, God?

Do I have an openness?
An acceptance?
A hope?
Or just a mere understanding?

My heart is open,
write your everlasting words upon it.
Guide my footsteps,
to the dawn of new Hope.

May I embrace,
every challenge.
May my eyes,
see your truth.

My knowing God,
fill me with your love,
wash me with purifying grace,
create in me a steadfast spirit.

And as I rest,
may I sort through,
my thoughts and understanding
growing ever closer to you, Lord.

Being First

What does be first mean?
Is this important?
Why did the disciples
argue over their place?

Does to be first mean greatest?
Does it mean importance?
Jesus reminds us that,
being first results in being last.

Jesus tells the disciples,
not only last of all,
but a servant to all.
What would your response be?

Jesus, you tell us to have a childlike faith,
a faith trusting and loving,
you gather children to yourself,
asking us to embrace them also.

May I embrace a childlike faith,
bringing me ever close to you,
having your arms surround me,
feeling the love of the Father.

Being a child,
puts me last,
but first in the eyes of God.
May I serve others always.

May my seat be,
the one of a servant,
not first,
but last.

Be My Witness

Be my witness,
Testify to the truth, my truth,
That I have come,
to restore everlasting life.

What would be your reaction?
How would you respond?
Would you recognize him?
How would you feel walking
on the road to Emmaus?

The empty tomb gives Hope.
You still aren't sure?
Jesus appears offering peace to all.
Thomas puts his fingers in the wounds.

Jesus has completed His mission.
Now we are charged with a mission.
How well are we doing?
Do we bring Jesus' "Good News" to others?

Let us reflect back on our Lenten journey?
Look at the climax of Holy Week.
Did Jesus not give you all that He promised?

Moving with Joy and Hope,
Let us pray for the strength to be a disciple,
Not afraid to encounter challenges,
But rest in the peace of Christ.

A Small Token

What can I give?
How much is enough?
Where do I draw my gift?
How is it measured?

Daily we are confronted,
decisions to be made,
discerning worth in life,
drawing conclusions.

What guides our decision?
What standard do we draw from?
Is enough, enough?
How does our self-offering measure up?

Look at the vulnerable,
do they give more?
Is their faith an example of character?
Do they model the behavior of a sincere disciple?

Who recognizes the true God?
Did the widow give more?
A "small token" drawn from all she had,
having no surplus to use.

Salvation was accomplished,
through a self-offering by Jesus Christ,
giving himself out of love,
an ultimate sacrifice for all.

Jesus gave only what he had,
knowing it was enough,
protecting the vulnerable,
being a source of love to all.

May we pray out of gratitude and mercy,
for the grace of integrity, generosity and love.

A New Day

A new day has dawned,
my spirit renewed,
my joy and thankfulness,
comes only from you.

I am thankful for this day,
an opportunity to grow in your love,
invite others to share in your hope,
and the wonder of your compassion.

It is your grace,
giving me another dawn,
a time to turn my heart to you,
a time to know you better.

What is there to gain without hope?
What is there to learn without your grace?
How can I turn my heart to you?
Where would I be without you?

The journey of life is not but mere steps.
It is entwined in the grace and hope of you,
a journey known only to you,
a time and space created for me.

Jesus,
each step is embraced with the love of you,
a companion and support,
a guide and mentor,
a friend and comforter.

May each day open wide my eyes,
to all the beauty you have created,
but more so,
your ever presence in my life.

A Mustard Seed of Patience

How often do we say?
If I only had taken the time,
if I only listened more,
and if I only didn't try to rush things.

Mustard seed-
you are so small in size,
but big in nature,
and strong in stature.

We wait and hope,
we pray and anticipate,
we watch and see,
we become anxious and frustrated.

Is our patience,
the size of the mustard seed?
Can we water and tend it?
Will it eventually grow?

God is in control,
He will bring forth the branches.
We can only be in "wonder and awe"
of God's greatness.

So, as we tend our mustard seed
of patience,
cultivate its future existence
by the "wonder and awe" of our Lord.

For all things are possible
on God's time, love and nurturing.

Trusting in Jesus

When the challenges of storms come your way.
What do you do?
Panic?
Try to control the storm?

God challenges us,
trust in me,
give it up to me,
be patient and turn to me.

How often do we think that we got it?
How many times do we lose our faith in God?
Do we say, "why me?"
Is it our time or God's time?

I pray,
we kneel at the foot of the cross,
trusting in the love and strength of Jesus,
placing our challenges before him.

Trust in Jesus,
let God work on His time,
be a patient and faithful disciple,
believing in the power of the cross.

Trust and follow,
Open your heart,
Reach for Jesus,
And know all will be well.

Spiritual Reflection

Light of Christ,
Embrace my heart,
Warm my being
Light my way.

Where are we?
Without you what can we do?
How can life make any sense?
Can we find our way without your light?

Days of darkness and despair
Brought to light by only you.
Comfort embracing our life
With your loving hands.

Secure and safe
Held close to your breast
Sharing in your loving ways
Offering forgiveness and a helping hand.

Moving to an understanding
Of the way of the light,
The closeness to each other
As we are close with you.

Reaching ever upward to your light,
Sharing your light
through a conversion of heart
being your hands and feet to one another.

Kingdom

Where is your kingdom?
Jesus said,
"My kingdom does not belong to this world."
Did the disciples and others understand?

Jesus' kingdom,
shocking and countercultural,
a force against evil,
suffered and crucified for truth.

Does your kingdom resemble His?
What stands foremost for you?
Do you believe in Jesus?
Do you believe in His kingdom?

In a world,
surrounded by much controversy,
filled with political and social issues,
being bombarded by everyone's truth.

Jesus, we call on you,
keep us steadfast in your truth,
arm us in your spirit,
support our thoughts and actions for good.

Jesus, you are alive,
feeding us today at Mass,
strengthening us for the battle,
your army against evil today.

Jesus,
as we testify to the truth,
may we continue to listen to your voice.

Inheritance of the Light

We are inheritance of the Light,
sharing in the Light,
only through our Baptism,
called to bring Christ's Light to others.

Could you drop everything?
Could you leave your new and best things behind?
Is living humbly difficult for you?
Do you believe being a disciple is counter-cultural?

Lord Jesus,
we know that humility,
brings a great reward,
an eternal salvation with you.

Our faith brings us closer to you,
a worker in the vineyards,
a Light in the darkness,
Peace and Consolation in distress times.

We open our hearts to you,
knowing you are the only one that satisfies,
the one to bring forgiveness and mercy,
a true gratification to our life.

May we walk in your Light,
be strengthened by your Body and Blood,
Comforted by your words,
Loved as the Father loved you, Jesus.

We pray, Lord, continue to nourish our flame,
strengthen us to be good disciples daily,
knowing our true inheritance of the Light,
comes in our promise of eternal life with you.

Do You Love Me?
You Ask?

You ask me, Lord,
"Do I love you?"
Just as you asked Peter,
three times on the shore.

How can I count the ways?
For this love I have for you.
You share yourself with me
Daily in prayer, guidance and light.

I experience your love in the Eucharist
And the word sent down in your teachings.
You are there,
in my challenges and trying times.

I see you in the faces,
of others I encounter each day.
In the poverty and devastation,
Your light of hope is there.

To ask me, "Do I love you?"
I would have to say yes without hesitation.
You bring comfort and warmth
Contentment and peace to my soul.

Your light is my way,
Your love is my comfort,
Your arms console me,
And you bring everlasting life to me.

Yes Lord, Jesus,
"I do love you with all my soul and being!"

I Ask You, "Who Do You Say That I Am?"

I search my soul,
Oh Lord,
just to answer your question,
"Who do you say that I am?"
I reflect on my thoughts,
I reflect on you,
I contemplate your life
and all that you are to me.

Your entrance as a child,
Your ministry as an adult,
Your lessons to be learned,
And your crucifixion for my soul.

Where do I begin to put into words?
Who you are to me,
A friend, a leader, a guide,
A teacher, a brother, a Savior.

You are the inner most of my being,
The heart of my life,
The silent whisper in my ear,
And the intimate words of faith that I speak.

You are the acts of justice
That I do,
My joys and sufferings
The beauty and light in the world.

May my heart embrace you
Through my conversion
On my journey of life.

What are you Looking for?

What are you looking for?
A question asked so many times in our life.
Do we ever come up with an answer?
Do we just ignore the question?

As we enter into a New Year,
listening is the art of opening up,
opening ourselves to others,
letting God into our lives.

Every day, we can wonder,
searching for many things,
hoping for happiness
looking for that which satisfies us.

In our search,
we experience anxiety and emptiness,
a lack of satisfaction,
the panic of not knowing.

Jesus listens for our wants.
Do we listen to His reply?
The disciples followed Jesus,
He asked them, "What are you looking for?"

Imagine the great feast,
the delight and joy
when we are open to the spirit,
guiding us from where we are
to where God intends us to be.

The Way of the Cross

What does the Cross mean to you?
Two bars intersecting together,
Joining the love of the Father,
To the Begotten Son,
With the Love between them.

Oh, Cross of Jesus,
you have taught us,
how to live,
and how to die.

You showed us,
how not to fear,
or suffer anxiety,
doubting not ever-lasting life.

In the midst, of your Cross,
we see Light,
we see Grace,
but above all we see your Love.

As we walk in Jesus' footsteps,
we walk the Way of the Cross,
carrying our own Cross.
knowing that we have done our part in faith, hope and love.

Waiting for Jesus with Love

During this time of "Waiting,"
we must learn to be patient,
as Jesus was patient with his disciples.

We see John the Baptist,
being patient as he awaits those
that are looking to repent and
the appearance of the anointed one.

We come to experience patience
through love of each other.
As our love grows,
So does our ability to be patient and forgiving.

So, as we wait for,
the second coming of Jesus Christ
Let our love grow,
as the Father's love is endless for us.

May we experience,
in a quiet reflection,
the love and patience necessary,
to Keep Watch and Be Alert.

The Last Word

As the sun rises,
You stand in the light of your Resurrection.
You walk the shore,
Waiting for your disciples to appear.

You walk not with feelings of betrayal,
Bitterness for the trial, torture or execution.
You did not let death have the last word,
But instead, life.

If we choose to believe in your Resurrection,
We choose to believe in life everlasting.
We choose to be compassionate,
Filled with love for God, our Father and each other.

On the shore,
You gave Peter a chance to redeem himself.
You asked, "Do you love me?"
As Jesus asked Peter,
So does Jesus ask us, "Do you love me?"

Image sitting with Jesus on this Resurrection morning,
Him asking you this question, "Do you love me?"
Responding, "Yes Lord, I love you in spite of my brokenness."
Jesus responding, "You are mine and I love you
and I will be with you to the end of time."

Strength to Forgive

Jesus, you showed us how to forgive.
Why do we struggle so?
We want to be like you,
and emulate you in our life-
especially in total forgiveness of others and ourselves.

Do we think ourselves as being better?
Do we struggle so because of pride?
Do we harbor bitterness and resentment in our hearts?
Are we like the mother bird protective of the hurt?

We pray, Lord Jesus,
to help us put aside all the obstacles of thoughts,
the feelings that block us from experiencing true forgiveness.
We pray,
for a humble heart,
the ability to lessen our pride
and to know there are many sides to hurt.

Lord Jesus,
as you looked down from the cross,
you asked your Heavenly Father to forgive them.

Did they not recognize you as their Lord of peace?
Were pride and being right the obstacles blinding their eyes?

We pray, Lord Jesus,
that as we grow in our love for you and faith,
we will grow with strength to readily forgive others.
We pray,
for a conversion of heart,
filled with strength, openness and forgiveness,
as we encounter challenges in our life.

Reflecting on You

Reflecting on you, Lord Jesus,
in the hard times.
As we struggle with the simplest task,
we reflect on your ministry.
Constantly you were challenged for your teachings,
Even today,
we struggle with accepting your truths.
You taught forgiveness
in the face of conflict and betrayal.
You taught love
in laying down your life for a friend.
You taught,
what we needed to do,
in order to enter into the Kingdom of Heaven
through the narrow gate.
You shared that
the Son of God must suffer and die
and your most trusted disciple could not accept this.
Your followers deserted you,
when you taught that for eternal life,
we must share in eating your body and drinking your blood.
We struggle with asking forgiveness,
from those that we have offended,
but more so forgiving those
that have offended us.
So, we pray,
may today bring a conversion of our hearts
to embrace your hard teachings.
May we be an instrument of these teachings,
as we are presented with our daily challenges.

Prayer of Discernment

Oh Lord,
thank you for all the lessons you have shown me.
You taught me how to love,
not just by words, but through your actions with others.

On the night you were betrayed,
you prayed earnestly to remain faithful to your Heavenly Father,
so that you would be able to complete your mission.
Your painful and discerning prayer
gives me the confidence to believe and trust also in our Heavenly Father.

Oh Jesus,
walk with me through my journey of discernment,
help me to see through your eyes,
let my actions be what your actions were in the face of betrayal.

I pray,
be with me when confronted with uncertainty,
help me to stay vigil in my darkest moments.
Lead me into your light and guide me,
so that I may see your way
and not be blinded by things of this world.

Jesus,
help me to be a wake to all you place before me,
to pray confidently,
for those that have no-one to pray for them,
urgently for those that are suffering,
patiently for those who do not understand,
and compassionately for those that are hurting from violence.

Heavenly Father,
I ask all of this through Jesus Christ, your Son, and the power of the Holy Spirit.

A Prayer for the Joy of Forgiveness

Heavenly Father,
through the obedience of Jesus,
who offered His Life in the service of all,
help me with Your Kindness.
Make me strong through the Eucharist.
May I put into action the saving Mystery
I celebrate in the Mass.
Forgiveness comes from the heart,
know as I extend my forgiveness to others,
peace will encompass their being.
Father, open my heart to all those I have offended,
wrap your loving arms around them,
comforting them as I move forward in love.
Protect me with Your Love
and prepare me for eternal happiness.
I know the joy experienced by forgiveness,
may I offer this forgiving peace to others.

Prayer for Eternal Life with God

Heavenly Father,
in glorifying Jesus
and sending us your Spirit,
You open the way to eternal life.
May my sharing in this Gift increase my love
and make my faith grow stronger.
Send Your Spirit to cleanse my life
so that the offering of myself to You at Mass
may be pleasing to You.
May my sharing in the Eucharist,
our Bread of Life,
bring me eternal life.

Strength From Jesus

Lord Jesus,
from your beginning the evil one has sought your mother,
so that you would not come into the world.
God, your Heavenly Father, protected her,
keeping her safe and His promise to all his creations.

As you stepped out into the light of your Baptism,
it was revealed to all present that
you were His Beloved Son,
and how pleased He was with you.

Lord Jesus, knowing the challenge ahead of you.
You sought solitude and mediation,
as you moved throughout the desert,
preparing yourself for all that was to come.

But the evil one,
sought you out,
challenging and tempting you,
offering bread, power and prideful gains.

As we reflect on your greatest challenge,
the cross,
may we pray for your strength as an example to all of us,
facing our daily challenges.

We pray,
may we measure the value of what we do and say,
by your cross, Lord Jesus.
May we know that we too participate in your saving victory,
over the evil one as we respond to you grace offered to us.

Holy Spirit,
the Advocate sent by you to us,
strengthen and give us courage as we trust in you to guide
our every decision.

A Passer-By

Lord Jesus,
I see the torture you have sustained for me.
Not a word had you spoken,
as insensitivity, rudeness, and unmerciful people jeer at you.

I look in your eyes,
I see your love and kindness.
I feel deep inside me your pain and anguish,
as you walk each step,
carrying the burden of my sins.

What can I do to lift the weight from your shoulders?
How can I help right the wrong?
Do we not understand?
Can we not feel your pain?

I am broken too,
I share and feel your pain,
I share in your burden today.
I look with regret upon your cross.

Lord Jesus,
I reach out to you for forgiveness.
I look for mercy and compassion,
deep in my soul.

I pray,
not to be just a passer-by,
but an instrument of your love and forgiveness
in the world today.

Look Down Upon Me

Lord Jesus,
look down upon me,
as I kneel at the foot of your cross.

Look deep into my soul,
as a created child of God.
Know the compassion and understanding,
I have for others.

I pray and beseech you,
to make me your instrument of hope,
a model of faith,
and an example of love in the world.

Even on the cross,
you looked down,
giving last words
for us to remember.

Lord Jesus,
always from your lips,
the word "Forgiveness".

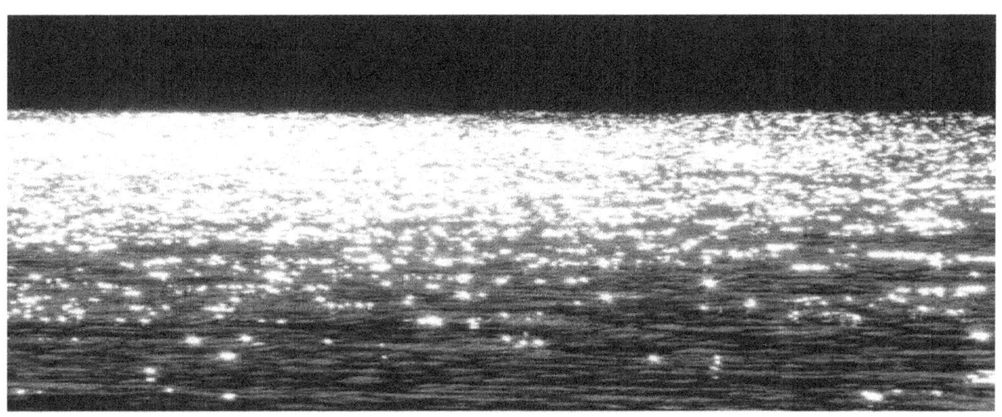

Living Water

Lord Jesus,
You promised that all who thirst
and hunger would be satisfied.
It is only through the "Living Water"
that you offer,
will our thirst be quenched.
You spoke to the Samaritan woman,
offering her the "Living Water"
and she recognized you as the Christ.
May we too,
recognize what you offer to us in the Eucharist,
the nourishment that satisfies our every desire.
Jesus,
you gave yourself for the life of the world,
by following your Father's will.
You are our Shepherd,
guide us toward the "Living Water" of life.
We pray,
each day may we be worthy,
to be satisfied by the food,
you offer for eternal life.

Become More Like Jesus

God, our Father,
You redeemed us
and made us Your children in Christ.
Through Him,
You have saved us from death
and given us Your Divine life of grace.
By becoming more like Jesus on earth,
may I,
come to share His glory in Heaven.
Give me,
the peace of Your kingdom,
which this world does not give.
By Your loving care,
protect the good You have given me.
Open my eyes,
to the wonders of Your Love
that I may serve You with a willing heart.

Hope

Lord Jesus,
As we journey with you,
walking side by side,
conversing about all the challenges today.

We reflect on the two disciples,
their journey to Emmaus.
Let us ponder,
what is different today?

Do we run from the conflicts?
When things do not go the way,
we want them.
Do we flee?
Wanting something so different.

The Resurrection!
The belief that death did not have the last word.
Let us open our hearts to the new Hope each year,
The power of you our Lord, Jesus Christ.

Oh Lord, Jesus Christ,
you have brought us your glorious Resurrection,
submitting to the Father's will,
carrying our sins to the cross,
so that we may continue to have Hope and
confidence in our Heavenly Father.

We ask, in these troubled times,
that we will experience you ever nearby,
hearing the words to lift us up,
and bring peace to our being

Strength and Guidance

Heavenly Father,
thank you for your faithfulness
throughout the generations.
Your word says that,
although people plan their course in their hearts,
it is you who establishes our steps.
Give me strength and guidance
for everything that lies before me.
Whatever I do today,
your loving eyes are on me
and you have promised to guide me.
Help me to fix my eyes
on you as I run the race of life.
Help me to walk by faith
and not by sight.
Strengthen me through your Holy Spirit.
Through Jesus Christ, our Lord.

Guiding Light

Light so bright,
Guide our way,
Bring us into your Light,
Out of the darkness.

Pointing tail of glow,
Telling us the way,
Revealing to us,
What the Light can show.

God's Light of love,
Lifting the shadows in our heart,
Opening up,
The way to Peace and Joy.

How can we spread the word of love?
How far will we go?
Let Jesus engulf your daily life,
Go the extra mile to discover him.

May the glow and guiding Light,
Bring you ever close to the love of God,
And embrace the tenderness and sweetness,
that only Jesus can offer each of us.

Following the Light

As you move along in your journey,
how will you follow the Light?
Will you let it guide you?
Will you try to direct the Light?

At this time of darkness and despair,
this Light will bring Hope,
a Hope and Joy not seen,
to many for a long time.

May the brilliance and illumination,
shine not only to light a darkened world,
but to warm and convert cold hearts,
drawing you closer to Christ, Our Savior.

A baby,
with such power and love,
gentleness and kindness,
wrapped and held in a wooden crib.

Let you take the time,
to let the Light,
empower you and convert you
as you gaze on the child.

May you follow the Light,
embracing the guided path,
allowing yourself to be reflective
and converted to the love of Christ
and one another.

Christ, Son of the Living God

Who would have thought,
you would come as one of us,
a tiny dependent human,
the Son of the Living God.

You desired to be close to me,
knowing my inner thoughts and false,
but loving me just the same,
forgiving my indiscretions.

You shared the way.
You shared the truth.
You shared your life with me,
even to the end on a cross.

You proved that you could triumph,
over the dark sided one,
rejecting his ways and offers,
and at the end conquering death.

You demonstrated forgiveness,
through your many teachings,
showing me how I could live
and love others as you love me.

May I embrace,
you're loving and forgiving nature,
calling on you in times of darkness,
and surrounding me with your consoling arms.
May I be to others as you have been to me.

Beckoning Hands

Hands so many hands!
Hands reaching forth,
hands smooth and tender,
large and callous,
crooked and swollen.

An ever stream of beckoning hands,
wanting to gather in the power,
the strength and beauty of spiritual
nourishment.

Oh, how the line continues,
young, old, middle age, tall, small,
peoples of all ethnic backgrounds.
Hand after hand.

Hands from all walks of life,
joining together for one purpose.
All in the same prayer and agreement
I believe, Amen, I believe,
In the living body of Jesus Christ,
Our Savior,
That I receive today!

What do I Have to Give?

Lord Jesus,
through my baptism, I share in your light,
I am called to share this light with
everyone I encounter in my life.

What do I have to share?
What skills do I have like the first disciples?
How can I too be a fisherman of many today?
Am I skilled as they were to gather others to themselves?

Reflecting on the first disciples,
"Did they really understand your message?"
I too wonder,
if I can understand what you ask of me.

So, I have gone back to your teachings,
"How do I treat my neighbor?"
Do I love others as I love myself?
Do I love God above all things?

Reflecting brings me to a threshold,
loving others comes with a great price.
A price you paid a long time ago.
that comes only through forgiveness and understanding.

May I be a channel of forgiveness and understanding,
A beacon in the darkness of despair,
A light in the shadows,
A hand reaching out to others.

May I bring peace and love
to a world in turmoil and despair.
May my actions help to bind the wounds,
and open the doors of uncertainty.

A Season of Waiting

As we reflect on the Advent season,
let us pray in this first week for hope,
a lasting light
to guide us all out of the darkness
as we await the birth of Christ.

As we move into week two
let us come together
in community and unity to pray for faith.
A faith unshaken
by any challenges presented to us
as we await the light of Christ in the darkness.

In week three,
let us celebrate the joy
of knowing the knowledge
that the light of Christ will bring
the world into a light
so bright that all darkness
will be illuminated by Christ presence.

At last,
we will experience the peace in week four
that radiates in the infant Jesus' birth
in Bethlehem
and the great star
leading all people to come to and share
in the beauty and peace of Christ's light.

May the Advent season
bring all of us
a strengthening
in our hope, faith, joy and peace experienced only
to us through the light of Christ
that we come to share in through our Baptism.
Let us light up the darkness in all the world
as we wait for Christ's second coming.

The Joy of Advent

As we reflect on the Joy of Advent,
we are called to action,
an action that brings acts of kindness, caring and love,
to a wilderness of deception, greed, abuse and hatred.

We as disciples of Jesus Christ,
crying out in the wilderness as John,
reminding others of the joy to come,
O Emmanuel, O Emmanuel.

In this season, we can testify to the light,
a light that will radiate and bring lasting peace,
a peace, the world has not seen,
the peace of Christ, a baby in a manger.

Oh Emmanuel, Light of Peace and Joy,
may we rejoice in knowing.
the Son of God will appear
bringing the everlasting light of peace and love to us.

Celebrate with Joy,
praising the Lord,
resting in His love
and sharing yourself as Christ light to others.

Peace on Earth

Every year,
you live in anticipation of,
what this season will bring.

You have hopes and prayers,
thoughts of years gone by.
The memories and joys,
the sorrows and visions of empty chairs
and quiet sounds and moments.

Your thoughts,
turn to the greatest gift,
the sounds that fill the air,
the moments that fill our heart every year.

As you sit,
you anticipate the greetings of others,
the friends and family,
the anticipation of joy on many faces.

As you reach out to each other,
may you keep in your heart the greatest gift of God,
Jesus Christ, His Son.
A baby,
wrapped in swaddling clothes,
his innocents and joy.

As you gaze upon Jesus,
May your heart swell up with love,
and challenge yourself
to be an instrument of peace on earth.

WWJD

We often see these four letters and wonder what do the mean?
They are simple letters that have at the core a powerful message.
What Would Jesus Do?

On the surface,
we could say that it is easy to answer,
but the underlying message is the action,
action we chose to do in our responses.

Jesus has served us all as a role model,
how he responded to the Pharisees,
as they continued to try and trick him with questions.

This is an important time to set aside,
all of our differences in our culture,
come to a call of action to bring God back into everyone's life.

Jesus would show mercy, compassion and love,
reaching out to each of us no matter who we are,
or where we live or who are parents are in the world.

Are we not a Catholic community,
strong advocates for understanding, mercy and love,
because we are all connect?

The cross is a living organisms attached to Jesus Christ,
we are the role models,
the hands and feet of Jesus in the world.

Our young people see and hear,
observe our actions,
questioning us about all things.

What would you say to them?

Problems Like Stones

We all have problems,
hard as stones,
unsurmountable,
tough to break them.

Are you being overwhelmed with problems?
Do you wonder where to turn?
Are these pulling you down?
Stones holding strong.

You need to look to the positive,
easily said,
difficult to do,
an endless process.

Reach out into all this darkness,
search for the light,
a light of hope,
resting within the cracks.

You will find the goodness when you search,
strength to lift you up,
climbing from under the pressures,
moving the darkness with courage.

Light separates the blind wall,
opening the cracks of light,
rays of revelation come pouring forth,
a new direction – a gift from a loving God.

The Earth, Sea, Sky
Proportional to Each Other

The earth gives us our birth,
only a beginning,
it starts so slow,
it's course to grow.

It instills life into that which does not exist,
a spark of life for eventuality.
The sea shall take the spark,
washing it about.

Life filled with endless fears and doubts,
but do not falter,
it will be altered by the currents of destiny.

The sky shall take the currents,
moving to a higher place of final resound,
it possesses all that has been created,
sweeping them to heaven with an endless bound.

To remain with He,
who first sought and now has found.

The Endless Struggle

Is everything we do in vain?
I can only say,
what we do will always remain.

It will live in the hearts of those,
who are nearby,
and in the hearts of those from afar.

We cannot measure our worth,
or the potentialities of all we do,
for it is not written or prescribed in our efforts,
it only comes forth in whatever we do.

We are often judged as being unfair,
by those that are critical,
but you see,
they are only cynical.

Life is as it has been for many years,
a long road,
an endless struggle,
remaining in the hearts of those,
who are so dear.

What Can I Give

For what can I give to you?
Is it something that will last?
Or shall it perish like the oncoming waves of the ocean?

Whatever it may be,
I want it to be something pure and something rare,
for so many things that are given,
are common – without true expression.

If I were to give you,
the salt of the ocean,
it would lack the water.

If I were to give you,
the earth,
it would lack the life,
it possesses.

For in the partialities of all things,
we lack the full meaning.

So, I shall give to you,
only peace of mind,
to obtain all that you can find.

Stairway of Awareness

If I were to call you,
from the depts of my mind.
Would you answer me and be kind?

May I,
but speak of need from my heart,
it has been there from the start.

In the valley of the multitudes,
your beauty displayed in attitudes.
In the mountains of emptiness,
your voice disclosed in peacefulness.

For in separation, we sought,
that which was in your depths to be caught.
I unaware of your presence,
and you oblivious to mine.

Each affecting,
one another,
through the stairways of time.

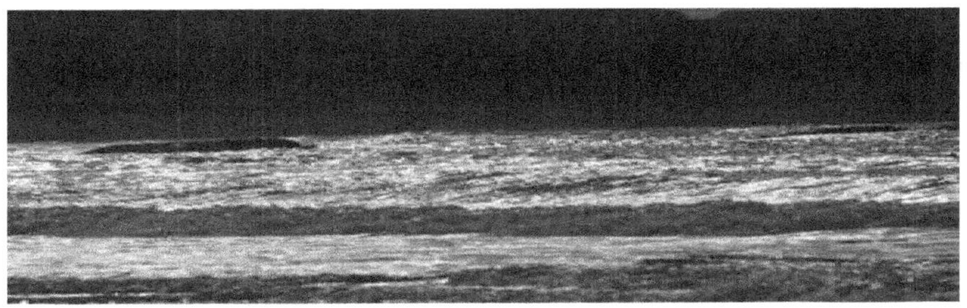

Storms of Confusion

Do you experience Storms of Confusion?
What are these?
Moments of helplessness?
A state of giving up?

Often, you experience moments,
days, in some instances,
feeling tossed and lost,
uncontrollable overwhelmingness.

Outside in the world,
merciless activities,
unavoidable despair,
darkness surrounding your every view.

You ask, "What is all this?".
A loss of focus on the positive,
storms of confusions,
bringing out the darkest corners.

You must look for the trust,
a proven peace maker,
the quieter of the storms,
faith in His ever presence.

We walk through a valley of darkness,
confusion and powerless feelings,
only when we lack trust,
a faith above the storms.

You reach out,
echoing the words,
"Save me",
Jesus will catch you – Trust in Him.

Why do you Fear?

Why do you fear?
Loud noises,
unprecedented sounds,
unrecognizable confusion.

You are blasted daily,
distracted,
uprooted in thought,
experiencing a lack of security.

You look around,
glancing at the hustle of movement,
disoriented from normalcy,
not knowing where to turn.

Your mind filling up,
erratic thoughts,
clarity lost,
time spinning out of control.

What causes this fear?
Evil surrounding you,
pulling at your mind,
draining you of calmness.

You experience this!
Do you not know you are not alone?
You have no need of fear,
Jesus is with you always – rest in Him.

Sharing the Gift

How do you feel when given a gift?
Do you hold it quietly?
Do you think of the content?
What is the bigger picture?

A gift given,
a special occasion,
uncommon timing,
hidden from view.

The question,
why?
What must you do?
Is it a gift to share with another?

Often surprised,
you receive a gift,
a treasure,
an offering from a notable power.

God offers a gift to you,
a small glance,
a view of something powerful,
a peek into God's kingdom.

How are you welcomed at the end of time?
Sharing God's gift with another,
bringing God's light and love into the world,
a small task with significant rewards.

Senses

What do you hear?
What do you see?
Do you fill your senses?
Absorbing that which is surrounding you.

You are bombarded by noise,
words with conflicting meanings,
tiny pieces picked from dialogues,
blown up into sorted content.

You see, doctored visions,
illusions of truth,
guided journeys of themes,
moments leading to a specified destination.

What fills your senses?
Confusion to say the least.
What is right?
Where will this all lead you?

You know,
good thoughts fall on knowledge,
uncertainty lives in shallowness,
abundance grows with fertile thoughts.

An open heart,
filled with love and compassion,
sorting through the noise,
bringing a calmness to your senses.

Live not in illusions,
embrace all truth,
gather knowledge,
rest in the depth of completeness.

What is You Burden?

What is your burden?
Perhaps, a challenge,
an unresolved dispute,
lack of compromise.

The question,
wisdom or intelligence,
an avenue to rectify,
solutions unfound.

Where do we turn?
Do we think the answers will come?
Knowledge and good judgment,
skills emitting a quality of wisdom.

Pondering inner thoughts,
succumbing to cultural arrogance,
stubbornness growing strong,
wisdom trapped in emptiness.

How do you lighten your burden?
A gentle nature,
humility of your heart,
thoughts of greater power.

Moving through life,
carrying burdens unresolved,
a worldly collar around your neck,
look to a greater world.

Resolve these burdens,
break the collar of despair,
reach for the glory,
a path filled with unconditional love.

What Sustains You?

What sustains you?
Where do you find support?
Who assists you in troubled times?
How do you lighten your burden?

Many questions,
filled with feelings,
lost thoughts,
various broken hearts.

Where do you turn in tribulation?
A great power exists,
a compassion and mercy,
a love beyond your feelings.

A prayer,
meditative moments,
eyes turned upward in the light,
a deep and soft sigh.

Are you called?
A moment of devotion,
a believer to love God,
feeling His importance above all things.

An assurance of His presence,
others sent out in anticipation of new life,
God sustains you with every step,
a refuge and trust in an infinite love.

Gather in family,
bring an uplifted spirit,
knowing the nearness,
a closeness to your listening God.

Are You Persistent?

You are challenged every day,
challenged by half answered questions,
uncertainty,
illusions created by your perspective.

Are you persistent?
What does it take to complete your challenge?
Do you read the signs correctly,
Is your exploration shallow?

You are quick to give up,
throwing your hands in the air,
seeing no solution to your challenge.
Is it easier to walk away?

Everyone needs assistance,
doors opening for an answer
positive results coming your way,
being open to receive the grace.

Persistence,
an avenue,
a skill to follow through,
a conclusion or resolution to your challenge.

If you want others to be generous,
offering assistance,
you too must be able to reciprocate,
offering your open mind and skills.

You are not alone,
the world offers many hands,
be confident,
put forth your needs to the love of Jesus.

A Mother

A mother is a special person,
one, who cannot be replaced.
As a child,
the first eyes I saw were mother's eyes,
the warmth felt, was mother's warmth,
tenderness bestowed to me from mother's care,
I knew some way she was special to me.

In youth, there was the rambling of affection from others,
but yet, there was a constant affection,
like a budding rose opening in blossom.
A vigil kept with loving eyes,
safe within the background,
they were mother's eyes.

In the cold fortress of solitude, there was warmth,
warmth seeping in as sunlight,
through the cracks in a wooden wall,
it was mother's warmth.

In the times of desertion and hardness,
I found tenderness,
a tenderness of sincerity
only found through mother's care.

Now, being older,
remembering the basic entities bestowed on me,
held within these has been your protectiveness,
always constant and secure.

All, I have known,
was given to me,
by you mother,
for you are very special to me.

A Dream

A walk into the naturalism of life,
the simplicity felt in the heartbeat of nature,
a joy of living in the breath of clarity,
movement in the chambers of shaded moments.

Reflection brought forth in my ever-constant ascension,
memories of moments in truth,
a truth displayed in the naturalism of beings,
time held constant with every echoing step.

Gazing out upon the pinnacles of spaciousness,
a remembrance of distant clouds in ideals,
thoughts stimulated by inner awareness,
awareness of a peaceful life.

A wandering through the ever-secluded beings,
the feeling of inner life,
moments paused through thoughtfulness,
the knowledge of being a part.

The outstretched arms of comfort,
a face of understanding care,
the overhanging of protectiveness,
the unspoken words were shared.

A silent pause of peace,
I turned an ear to listen,
the spoken words brought forth,
a moment in time held still.

I turned and walked away,
vibrations from my thoughts,
a dream of an ideal,
the vision, it was real.

A Course in Time

I have turned and travelled on into the distance,
leaving not with regret nor remorse,
thoughts only of the good for one's continuation,
the future of one's inner course.

I shall explore the ever-towering mountains,
walk among the warmth of the earth,
travel to the sand castles of the sea,
moments, enduring change as ceaseless waves on the shore.

I shall look under the overhanging branches,
turning my ears to the wind,
observe the natural without clouded eyes,
lifting them to the warmth of the sun

I shall wander not without direction,
my love of life will set the course,
ideals shall become realizations,
dreams shall become my being.

The mountains shall be the path,
the sun be the comfort,
life shall be the solitude,
my heart shall be the guide.

A Quiet Place

I have come to my favorite place today. It is a quiet place and unassuming in nature,
I sit upon the rocks, looking out over the vast space,
feeling the openness and silence contained here,
various colors weaving over the mountains -stimulate so many feelings inside.
It is mother nature's wardrobe, revealing emotions, letting us get close to her splendor in stillness
and silence. I wonder, closing my eyes, could I soar-
never touching down or feeling my body's suspension in space?
Could I be captured in the silence of suspended life – hung high in the sky overlooking the array
of colors? The silence brings back a more peaceful time in life.
As I sit here, I draw those memories out of this quiet place into the light as a child,
sitting and opening a special tiny box containing unique treasures collected each day.
As I reflect on each memory, examining them ever so closely,
feeling the comfort and warmth flow within and surrounding me.
In the comfort, I return to another place in time,
but only found through the avenues of my mind. I know, if I focus close,
I can feel the warm and tender hands that once held me and wiped the tears from my eyes.
The arms once surrounding and holding me with a silence of strength, protection and love
forever. A gentleness coming out of love and respect for one another with a bond not even
severed in death. This reassurance emerges and reaffirms the meeting together in a new life and
time. As I bathe in the warmth of memories so comes the overshadowing clouds of loneliness
and the reality of life. The loss develops out of the shadows and leaves an empty space inside.
Focusing on the reality, the tears swell inside me as the streams swell in a heavy rain and the
tears flow down my cheeks – damping my face and clothes.
It is only with time have I been able to hold the loss in this silent and quiet place.

Tears From the Soul of Life

A cloud felt sky,
pouring forth the tears of sorrow,
the open earth,
absorbing the sorrow in comfort,
droplets of emotions,
blanketing the soft earth,
a bed of solitude,
cushioning the strife.

The earth with outstretched arms toward the sky,
a face of salted tears,
moments in reflection of beings,
memories of peaceful giving.

The sky peering through tear trenched eyes,
emotions of eruption in sorrow,
an attempted movement toward the earth for tranquility,
a distant movement of the sky away in individuality.

The transition of contemplation for the cloud felt sky,
a realization of the earth in knowledge,
the understanding brought forth through the streams of life,
a comfort felt in the expulsion of sorrow.

Watching Over You

Remember me in the change of seasons.
Know my presence in the new life of spring,
the warmth of the summer sun,
the first crystal snowflake on your cheek in winter
and the bright vibrant colors of fall surrounding you.
Remember me in the quiet moments,
the rhythm of music,
my light humor and humble heart.
May my words bring you comfort.
When you look up at the vast sky,
see me in the ever-changing clouds.
Know that I am alive,
now, as your guardian angel
watching over you.

A Guardian Angel

I have walked in faith and love, now;
my journey is over.
Remember me by my joyous laughter,
endless sounds of music
and my open heart and tenderness.

My steps now are with the angels of heaven,
rejoicing in the heavenly choirs of song
and forever watching over you, day and night.
Let your tears wash away your sadness,
bringing a tender smile and memories of all my love.

In the quiet night, hear my soft prayers for you,
Know that I am there at dawn, shining in the day's sun.
I live, as a guardian angel for all those I love,
Reach out and you will feel my forever presence.

The Community of Faith

Lord Jesus, look upon your community of faith,
guide us and strengthen us,
as we become imitator of you in the world.

May we always remember,
all of our blessings
and may we share them with others.

We pray,
you will gather us together,
to listen to you through the Gospel message,
receive you in the precious Eucharist,
and go to be disciples in our community.

We know deep in our hearts,
You are the Truth, The Way and The Life,
Our path to eternal life.

Harmony in Existence

Harmony is the giving of two elements,
sharing in a union.
It is the existence of being,
expressing the feelings of an inner need.

It is the swaying of the trees,
in rhythm with the soft breeze,
the warmth of the fields,
covering the earth.

It is the living of mankind,
in a peaceful world.
Harmony is the togetherness of two people,
sharing in a friendship.

Friendship existing through communication,
understanding and kindness,
guiding direction and truth,
through the reality of time.

It is a survival,
blending birds of the wind,
with the vastness of the sky.

A blending of nature,
with a human element of imperfection.
Harmony is the transition of the fog,
the clouds of ideals,
and the earth of reality.

Eternal Time

I have walked a path alone,
a direction imposed upon my journey,
a path no-one can ponder upon,
this path unique to me alone.

I shall swing my sails into the wind,
feeling the freshness of rebirth upon my face,
the clarity of distant shores shall lie before me,
and the waves of constant motion ushering me forth.

If by chance, I turn, to the pinnacle of the sky,
I shall only reflect for a moment,
for through the towering mountains, I shall hold my reservations,
and the unique feelings of ideality will remain there upon the cloak of greenness.

Upon my salt covered face of the ocean,
I shall live in the novelty of a changing life,
capturing the shallowness as well as depth,
building momentary sand grain castles on the shore.

If for a moment, I visualize reflections of once formed sand castles,
I shall not alter the tide,
the destination lies in the hands of eternal time,
with the ebb of the ocean, filtering through the grains of a sand.

I shall not pause in the shadows,
nor shall I move in illusions of oncoming winds,
I shall live by my heart and the forthcoming winds,
my sails shall be filled with a steady course.

As I gaze upon the distant shores,
I shall meet them with a freshness of being,
the once clouded haze shall disappear with a restoration of clarity,
my being shall be felt in the softness of the off shore breezes.

A Moment's Pause

I shall turn my face to the wind,
I shall feel the windswept movement upon my face,
I shall not look back,
Nor ponder the paths I have travelled.

I shall find familiar sounds upon the shore,
as the ocean brings forth its salty spray,
in the fog felt ocean's early morin.

I shall see the ever-clearing sun upon the horizon,
as I walk upon the sand covered ground,
I shall not turn to see my steps wash away,
as I set my course in a forward direction.

I shall move upon the grains of sand,
if I hear a voice from reflections.
I shall not turn,
For only images of what was will be seen in the curling waves.

If by chance, there are steps by mine,
I shall only have to look to one side.
if the images become real, the steps will walk with me,
I shall not have to turn.

If a moment of time stands still,
I shall continue so not be caught in the web of suspension,
for time will not pause for anyone,
I shall move into infinity.

As We Grow Older

We meet many in our life,
some make us grateful,
others bring us strife,
few give us comfort.

As we grow older,
our eyes become keen to others,
we look only for the good each possess.

Not bitterness hardens our hearts,
putting asunder all misguided ways of the past,
allowing for the light of understanding to shed upon us,
brightening all the shadows of darkness found in confusion.

You find an extended hand reaching,
encountering a warm clasp and thankful smile
You learn fortitude through solitude,
patience through forgiveness,
love through eternal friendship.

The Changing Tide

The tide has turned,
all the clarity of being has become real,
the fog has lifted,
the waters are what they appear to be.

I standing upon the sand covered shore,
gazing out upon the glimmering ocean,
seeing many things that before have gone unnoticed.

In the ever-changing waves, I have found consistency,
the soft tender rolling whispers and echoes peace to my ears,
the spaciousness has revealed the freedom of life.

I have placed my hand upon the sand,
experiencing warmth within the grain's particles,
touching each changing segment,
building not a castle to be washed away.

A stroke of a finger from my hand,
engraving the significance found within this land,
it reads the following message,

"When the tide has turned, it washes the confusion from the light.
The warmth of the light renews the truth and trust of the earth,
the earth cleansed in a new revelation of brightness,
offering comfort in a vast spaciousness of freedom."

I turn, placing one foot in front of another,
moving on through time and destiny,
pausing for a moment,
looking over my shoulder.

What is seen?
All thoughts engraved upon the grain covered shore,
now, washed into the destiny of the ever-changing tide.

A Vision in Thought

Thoughts of you came into existence today,
thoughts pressing through the stillness,
reflections of moments vibrating throughout my being,
visions of you dispersed among the tree groves within the woodland.

I paused from my endeavors,
turning, I heard the soft whispers of your voice,
I knew it to be the echoing moments,
thoughts within me.

The images encountered there,
products of my thoughts,
existing to be real only in moments,
temporary and swift.

Lifting my eyes toward the clouded sky,
only the gray was real,
the blue lost among the clouds of darkness,
the sun's light smothered within the darkened sky.

All creating a severance and disappearance of you,
thoughts lost,
not knowing if I shall ever be with you again,
leaving empty thoughts in the hole of loss.

Reunification

I have come to stand by the open window,
far searching was my sight,
encompassed all the motion in stillness,
seeking out the distant light.

The fog was heavy within me,
a light pierced the darkened sky,
sitting and wondering why?

The rivers overflowed within my soul,
my touch was one with the day,
a barren waste,
I clenched a fist and sighed.

Inside, an ardent feeling struggled to survive,
my mind fell into reflections,
I peered beyond the pinnacles,
the clouds of ideality hung about,
I knew this feeling I was without.

In my hands, holding the emptiness,
as the earth would be without life,
my heart I harbored the solitude,
as a child lost in the night.

As a pillar resting on my brain,
I closed the window,
moving away,
I sat and thought – should I stay?

The wind ushered in a welcome sound,
an end to a search for all that was lost,
now, has been found.

Deep Truth

Do you experience *Deep Truth*?
Are there "aha moments" in your day?
Moments made clearer,
certain realizations ushered forth.

Do you struggle with understanding?
Consequences revealed through truth,
obscured views,
blurred notions.

What makes you see clearer?
A gift given to you,
eliciting beautiful thoughts,
a better perception.

You were infused with a gift,
guiding your thoughts,
sorting out the *Deep Truth*,
leading you through the difficulties.

This gift opens your heart,
welcoming in uncertainty,
clearing murky images,
discovering a sure path.

Faith infused in your soul,
fortified by prayer,
assisting in discerning the *Deep Truth*,
revealed not by you alone.

In the Quiet Night

I came to sit by the water's edge,
my mind wandered in thoughts,
as the fog drifted upon the silent shore,
many reflections emerged into view.

As I gazed upon the water's surface, I saw reflective stars,
the scattering of thoughts brought me back,
moments of shivering visions encumbering my being,
like the dew of the evening settles upon the blades of grass.

Thoughts brought many reflections,
visions reflecting upon the peaceful waters,
once held secure behind closed doors,
as life is sheltered in the darkened water.

Life from within pushed the darkness from these reflections,
a clarity of a reflecting entity of heaven.
Tears of joy, flowed into the undisturbed waters,
as I paused in turning away.

I knew, the many reflections must remain secure in a bond,
all that has gone before,
must remain within a cavern of silence,
as the depth of the waters remains undisturbed at night fall.

An Unforgotten Mark

A river of force flowed throughout all entities,
emerging forth came life,
carrying miles of fortitude in understanding,
the pulse was deep, the time was short.

An emergence of clarity arose within it,
a seemingly timeless moment,
held secure in the grips of strength,
one of tenderness eliciting a light of brightness in confusion.

A joining of weakness into uncontrolled power,
yet, a flowing in smoothness and softness,
a tender caressing of the hardness,
a molding of shapes from shapelessness.

The moment ran into an endless seizure,
the changing of creation in destruction,
a loss of thought into thoughtless actions.
movements resulting in unending turmoil.

Creations being carried in unknowing destinations,
the coming of a greater power,
replacing the peaceful flow,
separating each into rightful parts.

A soft hand in towering strength,
leaving an unforgotten mark.

A Pause – Why

I have often paused to wonder why,
gazing up toward the sky,
turning to the earth secure,
looking into waters crystal pure.

I have pondered the earth,
perhaps, in search of many things,
I have drifted up into the clouds,
learning much from what I have found.

I have been bounced on the water's edge,
watching sand grain castles curl and bend.
I have lost myself in the natural,
descending into the aspirations of simplicity.

Through the long search of being,
I have turned to look under each rock,
lifting each branch, wading in each stream,
soaking my being in each entity.

Now, a part has been explored,
I need not sit upon the shore,
nor turn my eyes toward the sky,
for I pause, but wonder not why.

A Beginning

In the stillness of early morin,
a sound broke the silence of night,
the sound brought the light,
the light, a new beginning.

The darken shadows disappeared,
light filling every corner,
a breath of new life,
a day encumbered with hope.

As the shadows faded in a transition,
the clarity of color is renewed with vividness,
the heart of life beats ever do steadfast,
and the echoing silence moves into motion.

The sky forms a blanket of blue,
a ground in which the clouds and sun play upon,
the rays reach out their arms to hold life,
welcomed into the warmth of their bosom.

As the clouds soften,
the bed of comfort emerges,
a new birth of hope is renewed within my being,
a new beginning.

Weeping Willow

Oh, weeping will,
forever flowing free,
your long-draped arms,
crying in ecstasy.

They try to satisfy you,
only harming you,
not understanding your hunger,
contained deep under.

You reach for the cool,
extending yourself toward,
a warmth of the soft land,
trying to take it in your hand.

The water comes so close to soothe,
trying to revive,
what you may lose.

You weeping willow will be loved,
by all,
who watch you tower,
reigning above them all.

Rough Waters

There is a constant motion,
movement not controlled,
a rising and settling,
an illusion underneath of calmness.

How do you weather the rough waters?
Do you come prepared?
Are you lured in by the constant sound?
Can you feel the power of the third wave?

Is life not the same?
Things come in threes,
the last compounding the other two,
a climax of sort.

You look to draw on your tools,
a chest full of wisdom,
experiences once challenged,
moments of drawn conclusions.

You draw deep from within,
pulling out,
laying the elements on the table.
What should you do?

You melt into the rough waters,
finding familiarity,
grabbing hold,
breathing deep and relaxing.

You know there is something more powerful,
an entity beyond your comprehension,
reaching down,
quieting the rough waters.

You wonder why,
a special quietness surrounds you,
a gentle heart embraces you,
a constant love sustains you.

In the Universe

How do you fit in the universe?
A small dot?
A speck almost seen?
A mite swirling in the air?

What is important?
Your size or your thoughts?
Feelings transformed into deeds,
Belief realized through grace.

You are invited,
You respond with trust,
New horizons open before you,
You are blessed.

You are created again,
Ascending to a soaring height,
Free from all that holds you back,
Delivered from prisons of fear.

Let go!
Be strong and welcome in the just,
Abundant grace will transform you,
Showing you an unyielding spirit.

Whoever believes,
Will not die,
This is promised to you,
A life in the vast universe.

You are called,
"Come out",
Respond to this call to life,
This new life with Christ.

Majestic Port

You stand with such strength towering above all,
surrounded by an endless silence,
beckoning to all.
For years, you have welcomed,
embracing all that come,
bringing solitude and reflection.
The constant rhythm that surrounds you,
lulls your guests into quietness,
eliciting a peaceful joy,
a sense of well-being.
Birds serenade, giving rise to special melodies,
turtles share the grounds,
laying deposits of life.
There is a sweet fragrance,
spread throughout your grounds,
guest smile and recall,
the sights and sounds.
How long have you stood proud?
Cared for by earthly angels,
being guides and directors for you,
nurturing many minds and spirits.

A port you have been for many,
an anchor in the turmoil of life,
a fortress of tranquility,
a temporary peaceful resting site.
So, as we salute you,
Majestic Vision and Port,
know the hearts you have changed,
memories living on in your vision.

Acknowledgement

First, I must thank God that endowed me with a gift to express myself and share hopefully motivational and spiritual life thoughts. We are all challenged and need assistance to discern a solution that is amicable to all we encounter. The Holy Spirit has whispered in my ear constantly to complete this manuscript to share my journey reflections with others. We are designed to live in community and support each other in whatever way we can do this. I pray, you will find a thought, you can reflect on that will assist your discernments.

The beautiful and fulfilling family life driven by two wonderful individuals, my parents, have encouraged me always to be who I was called to be in life. They were always there encouraging, supporting and loving me. My dearest friend, Marth, that encouraged me to write again, always a support in my endeavors and sounding board for the words of my reflections.

The many individuals supporting and encouraging me to publish my reflections. My hat is off to them for taking the time to read my work weekly in our bulletin. You all have been a very motivational audience and I thank you for this.

To life, itself, that teaches us many lessons. We are call to be challenged, but the end results are what we learn in order to grow into better people. It is a hope that we grow with each resolution that calls us to reflect even deeper. There are many twists and turns presented to us every day that calls us to pull out our arsenal of life tools. I hope, I have presented some food for thought that will assist you to discern a positive resolution for you.